CHILE PEPPERS

Hot Tips and

Tasty Picks for

Gardeners and

Gourmets

Beth Hanson
Guest Editor

FOR THE
ADVANCE
MENT OF
BOTANY
AND THE
SERVICE OF
THE CITY

BROOKLYN
BOTANIC
GARDEN
PUBLICATIONS
· MCMXCVIII ·

Janet Marinelli
SERIES EDITOR

Jane Ludlam
MANAGING EDITOR

Bekka Lindstrom
ART DIRECTOR

Mark Tebbitt
SCIENCE EDITOR

Handbook #161
Copyright © Winter 1999 by the Brooklyn Botanic Garden, Inc.
Handbooks in the *21st-Century Gardening Series,* formerly *Plants & Gardens,*
are published quarterly at 1000 Washington Ave., Brooklyn, NY 11225.
Subscription included in Brooklyn Botanic Garden subscriber membership dues ($35.00 per year).
ISSN # 0362-5850   ISBN # 1-889538-13-2
Printed by Science Press, a division of the Mack Printing Group.
Printed on recycled paper.

• TABLE OF CONTENTS •

INTRODUCTION

BETH HANSON

THE PARTNERSHIP BETWEEN people and the chile pepper is thousands of years old. In the latest phase of this partnership, electronic correspondence and commerce and modern marketing techniques all play parts. For years, a group of chile pepper devotees who called themselves "chile-heads" exchanged e-mail with recipes, tips for growing the hottest chiles, and help in finding the spiciest salsas. The number of aficionados grew, and, simultaneously, ethnic foods have become part of the American mainstream. More and more people developed a craving for chiles. Manufacturers and their marketing people found that chiles are an appealing design element and put them on mugs, tie racks, kitchen clocks, and strings of Christmas tree lights. Chiles crossed over, in a big way, into popular culture. On the Internet—a great place to gauge what's "hot"—you'll find the "Ring of Fire," a group of related web sites offering not only every variation on hot sauce and products like chile pepper cookie cutters, but also a huge variety of seeds, seedlings, and gardening information. Would-be purveyors of hot sauces and chile paraphernalia can even attend the "College of Chile Knowledge" every year in Albuquerque, New Mexico.

But chile peppers transcend the current trend. Whether or not Americans keep buying chile pepper posters and eating nachos and salsa, chiles

Chiles are vitamin and mineral powerhouses, and are rich in fiber.

will go on firing up the foods of people from Peru to Pakistan, as they have for centuries. Indigenous Americans first domesticated chiles about 7,000 years ago. Then, in the fifteenth century, Columbus "discovered" chiles, and they quickly traversed the globe on trading ships, finding a permanent place in foods everywhere they landed. On their travels, for example, they stopped in Korea and were incorporated into the fermented vegetable dish called kimchi. Koreans eat a lot of kimchi—and now they eat more chiles than any other people in the world: Chiles account for 12.5 percent of the daily food intake of the typical South Korean. The Turks brought chiles to the Balkans, where people bred them to reduce the pungency and to adapt them to the short growing season. In the form of paprika, chiles came to provide the color and flavoring of the Hungarian dish, goulash. Portuguese traders brought a few chile pods to India, giving curries of that part of the world their special flavor and pungency. Chiles are now essential to the cuisines of Asia, Africa, the Americas, and even parts of Europe. A quarter of the population of the globe eats hot chiles every day.

Chiles traveled round the world and were readily embraced for good reasons: They are vitamin powerhouses, each one packing more vitamin C than an orange. They are also rich in potassium, beta carotene, and fiber. And chiles contain compounds that some believe prevent cardiovascular disorders, certain forms of cancer, and cataracts. Their physiological power is evident to anyone who has consumed hot chile peppers in some form: The heart starts to beat rapidly, salivation and sweating increase, the nose begins to run, and the gastrointestinal tract goes into overdrive. To shut off the pain signals from the tongue, the brain secretes endorphins, the opiatelike substances that block pain. This experience may not sound like one to seek out again and again—but we do. Perhaps it's those endorphins that keep us coming back for more.

This book is a celebration of both the staying power of the chile in the world's gardens and cuisines, and of Americans' current enthusiasm for chiles. In the following chapter Paul Bosland, one of the world's preeminent pepper breeders, writes about the remarkable history of the chile and its journeys. Bosland is also the author of the "Encyclopedia of Chiles," (page 68), which includes more than 50 varieties, with tips on growing and preparing them, and ratings of how hot they are. In an extensive chapter on the pests and diseases that afflict chiles, Bosland discusses diagnosing and treating just about anything that may attacks chiles in gardens across the United States. Chile expert Doug Dudgeon spells out the basics of growing chile peppers, from germinating seeds to when and how to harvest. Susan Belsinger, chef, photographer, and writer, explains the best ways to preserve your chiles after the harvest, whether it's by pickling, drying, or freezing them. You'll also find a variety of recipes, from the savory to the sweet—and almost all pungent. Finally, you'll find the sources for the best selections of chile seeds and expert advice.

THE HISTORY OF THE

CHILE PEPPER

PAUL BOSLAND

THE CHILE IS MOVING OUT of the shadow of its sidekick, the tomato, to become a staple crop in the garden. New colors of bell peppers, which have always been popular with gardeners, sweet and mild jalapeños, novel ornamental types, and exotic chiles from around the world are inspiring new interest among gardeners. Fiery foods from ethnic cuisines are gaining influence, accelerating the popularity of chiles in cooking and in the garden. And because fresh chiles are "fat free, saturated-fat free, very low sodium, cholesterol free, low in calories, high in vitamin A, and high in vitamin C," according to the U.S. Food and Drug Administration, they make great additions to a healthy diet.

Chiles have not only a bright future but also a fascinating past. Chiles belong to the genus *Capsicum* and the Solanaceae or nightshade family. This large tropical family includes the tomato, potato, eggplant, and petunia. Chiles may be called peppers, but they are not related to *Piper nigrum*, the source of black pepper, nor are they related to the Guinea pepper or grains of paradise, *Aframomum melegueta*. So why the confusion in the name? Originally, chiles were found only in the Americas. But when Columbus searched for a shorter route to the East Indies and its prized spices, he found in the Caribbean a plant that mimicked the pungency of black pepper. He called it red pepper, probably assuming the pungent fruits were a new type of pepper, and introduced it to Europe. In 1493, Peter Martyr wrote that Columbus brought home "pepper more pungent than that from the Caucasus" [black pepper]. Chiles spread rapidly along the established spice trade routes from Europe eastward to Africa and Asia, where today they are major crops.

Most people are not adventurous when it comes to foods—we simply do not eat unknown foods. Yet this new food, unlike the introduced tomato and potato, was accepted and integrated into the cuisines of Europe, Africa, and Asia without hesitation. Perhaps people assumed, as Columbus did, that this plant was a form of black pepper, which was affordable only by the nobility. Now the peasants could grow pepper and flavor their dishes just as the wealthy did.

Chiles diffused throughout Europe, and by the sixteenth century were grown in Italy, France, and Germany. In about 1560 they arrived in Hungary, and became the famous Hungarian paprika. Centuries later, paprika was the source of a discovery that led to a Nobel Prize. Hungarian scientist Albert Szent-Györgyi, while working at Szeged University in 1931, isolated pure vitamin C, ascorbic acid, from tomato-shaped paprika. He had originally worked with the adrenal glands of cattle, but they contained such small amounts of the unknown material that he made little progress. Szent-Györgyi later described the discovery this way: He did not like the paprika dish his wife had prepared one evening, and told her he would finish eating it in his laboratory. Well, as they say, the rest is history—by midnight of that same night he knew he had found a treasure trove of vitamin C. In 1937, he got the call from the Nobel committee.

CHILES GO TO AFRICA AND ASIA

The cuisine of an area reflects, in part, the influences of its explorers, conquerors, and commercial contacts. Before chiles arrived in Africa and Asia, people there were already familiar with fiery spices. For centuries, they had used ginger, black pepper, mustard, melegueta, cloves, and other spices to season their foods. Then, during the sixteenth century, the Portuguese colonized Brazil, and subsequently introduced *Capsicum chinense* and *C. frutescens* into western Africa and the Congo basin. The shameful activities of slave ships from numerous countries were also responsible for introducing chiles to Africa, as exchanges between the Americas and Africa were common. Chiles were probably introduced into Asia by traders from Europe and Africa, and quickly became a major spice there, eventually dominating the cuisines of India and China.

No one knows for sure why chiles became a staple spice in the cuisines of Africa and Asia, but chiles did grow well there, and in many areas became a "subspontaneous crop"—it grew and replanted itself without human help. So here was a spice that was easy to grow, healthy,

Chiles are native to South America but are now used in cuisines worldwide.

Spanish paprika is one of the many chiles that brought new flavors to European tables.

and tasty. Nevertheless, perhaps chile became popular in both Asia and Africa for the same reason it became popular in the Americas: It enhanced the flavor of foods. When people added chiles to dishes, they became newly aware of the flavors of their customary foods. Just as wine, invented by the Romans, was appreciated by people all over the world, chiles may have been desired for the unique and exquisite flavors they provided. Many people argue that pungency is one of the five basic tastes, along with salty, bitter, sweet, and sour.

China, India, and Pakistan are now the world's three largest producers of chiles. Nowadays, it is so common to think of India curry or Szechuan dishes flavored with chiles, that it's hard to believe that they were completely unknown there just 500 years ago. Chiles were so quickly incorporated into the foods of Asia that in the 1700s a French taxonomist mistook China for the origin of one of the species, and called it *Capsicum chinense*.

TAMING THE WILD CHILE

The earliest chile breeders were the indigenous peoples of the Americas, who had emigrated from northern Europe 10,000 to 12,000 years ago; chiles were one of the first plants that they domesticated and cultivated.

CHOCOLATE CHILE PECAN BROWNIES

These rich chocolate brownies have a surprising, hot zing when you bite into a chile-covered pecan—the intensity of the chocolate works well with the chile flavor and sort of masks its heat. You are left with a rather pleasant "hot buzz" on the back of the tongue. We used a hot, ground red chile to make this recipe. If you are using a medium-hot, ground red chile, perhaps you should add an extra teaspoon to the batter.

¼ **cup water**
2 **tbsp. sugar**
1 **tbsp. coarsely chopped pecans**
1 **tbsp. hot ground red chile [to coat pecans]**
¼ **tsp. salt**
4 **oz. unsweetened chocolate**
10 **tbsp. unsalted butter**
1½ **cups sugar**
3 **extra large eggs**
1¼ **tsp. pure vanilla extract**
1 **cup unbleached flour**
2 **tsp. hot ground red chile [for batter]**
Generous pinch of salt

In a small skillet combine the water and the sugar and stir over medium heat for 2 minutes. Add the pecans and stir well with a wooden scraper as the water evaporates. After 3 or 4 minutes add the ground chile and salt and toss well to coat the pecans evenly. Continue stirring for a few minutes more until all the water is evaporated, the pecans are coated, and the pan is dry. Turn the nuts onto a plate or wax paper to cool.

Preheat the oven to 350°F. Generously butter and lightly flour a 13 × 9 baking pan. Melt the chocolate and the butter together in a heavy-bottomed pan over low heat or in a heat-proof bowl in the microwave. Stir well and let cool a few minutes. Beat the butter and chocolate mixture with a wooden spoon until blended. Stir the sugar in and mix well.

Beat the eggs and the vanilla into the batter until well blended. Stir in the flour, ground chile, and salt until just mixed. Stir in the pecans and pour the batter into the prepared pan, spreading it evenly.

Bake for 25 to 30 minutes, until a tester comes out clean. Cool in the pan on a rack, cut into pieces, and serve.

From The Chile Pepper Book *by Carolyn Dille and Susan Belsinger, Interweave Press, 1994. Reprinted with permission of the authors.*

CHILE PEPPER RECIPES

In the 1500s, the Portuguese brought habaneros and other chile peppers to Africa.

And chiles were not domesticated just once. There are five different domesticated species of chiles, so we can infer that they were domesticated at least five times, independently. The most likely ancestor of *C. annuum*—the species most extensively cultivated around the world today—is the wild chile piquín (*C. annuum* var. *aviculare*). It has a wide distribution, from South America to southern Arizona. Over millennia, Native Americans patiently selected and developed many of the pod types of chiles we know today from the chile piquín, including jalapeño, serrano, pasilla, and ancho, to name a few.

By the time Columbus arrived in the Americas, the Aztecs were growing not only the jalapeño, pasilla, ancho, and serrano, but the arbol and the mirasol. The sixteenth-century Spanish chronicler Fray Bernardino de Sahagún wrote that in the Aztec market there were "hot green chiles, smoked chiles, water chiles, tree chiles, flea chiles, and sharp-pointed red chiles." He noted that the Aztecs classified chiles into six categories based not only on level of pungency (high to low), but also on the type of pungency (sharp to broad). To further illustrate the importance of the flavor differences among the different chile types, Bernardino de Sahagún described how each was used in dishes—"frog with green chile, newt with yellow chile, tadpoles with small chiles," and so on.

The wild chile piquín is the most likely ancestor of many contemporary chiles.

The Aztecs found other uses for chiles. Among the paintings in the Mendocino Codex—a visual record of Aztec life—is a picture of a father punishing his 11-year-old son by making the boy inhale the smoke from dry chiles roasting on the hearth. Many police departments in the United States have found chile vapors to be equally effective against unruly criminals: They issue pepper spray to the officers on their forces.

To the first inhabitants of the Americas, chiles possessed mystical and spiritual powers. The Aztec, Maya, and Inca held chiles in such high regard that they withheld them from their diets when fasting to earn favors and to please the gods. Incas worshipped the chile as a holy plant, and considered it to be one of the four brothers of their creation myth, wrote Garcilaso de la Vega in 1609 in his *Royal Commentaries of the Incas*.

POTENT MEDICINE

Because of their unique pungency, chiles were used for more than just food or spice in pre-Columbian times. The wild chile fruits were first used as a medicine. Mayas used them to treat asthma, coughs, and sore throats. The Aztecs and the Mayas mixed chile with maize flour to produce *chillatolli*, a cure for the common cold. It was reported that the Aztecs placed a drop or two of chile juice on a toothache to stop the pain.

Today, the Jivaro of South America continue the practice by applying the fruit directly to a toothache. A survey of the Maya pharmacopoeia revealed that chiles are currently included in a number of herbal remedies for a variety of ailments of probable microbial origin. In Colombia, the Tukano tribe uses chiles to relieve a hangover. After a night of dancing and drinking alcoholic beverages, the Tukanos in Colombia pour a mixture of crushed chile and water into their noses to relieve the effects of the festivities. The Teenek (Huastec) Indians of Mexico use chile to cure infected wounds. The chile fruit is rubbed into the wound and can produce pain so severe that the patient passes out. The Teenek believe that the chile kills the brujo (evil spirit) causing the illness. They put red crushed fruits on their feet to cure athlete's foot fungus and consume a drink made from from boiled green fruits to cure snakebite.

Today, chiles are among the most widely used of all natural remedies. Creams made with capsaicin from chiles are the most recommended topical medication for arthritis: At nerve endings a neurotransmitter called substance P informs the brain that something painful is occurring. In reaction to chile's pungency, more substance P is released. Eventually, the substance P is depleted and fewer messages are sent from the nerve endings. As the level of available substance P is reduced, long-term inflammation—which can cause cartilage to break down—also dies down. Mastectomy patients and amputees suffering from phantom limb pain apply creams containing capsaicin to reduce postoperative pain. And prolonged use of these creams has also been found to reduce the itching that dialysis patients experience, pain caused by shingles (Herpes zoster), and cluster headaches.

And chiles have other physiological benefits. They are an important source of vitamins and many essential nutrients. The antioxidant vitamins A, C, and E are present in high concentrations in various chile types. In addition, chiles provide high amounts of vitamins P (bioflavonoids), B_1 (thiamine), B_2 (riboflavin), and B_3 (niacin). Chiles are richer in vitamin C than the usual recommended sources, such as citrus fruits. A green chile (medium-sized bell pepper) pod contains about six times as much vitamin C as an orange. In many diets, chiles are an important source of the provitamins alpha-, beta-, and gamma-carotene, and cryptoxanthin, which are transformed in the human digestive tract into vitamin A. The daily vitamin A requirement is met by consumption of one-half tablespoon of red chile powder.

CHILES TODAY

People around the world today eat chiles as a fresh vegetable or in their dehydrated form, as a spice. In many households, chiles are the only spice used to enhance an otherwise bland diet. By volume, pungent and nonpungent red chile products are among the most important spice com-

In pre-Columbian times, people first used chiles, such as wild chiltepin, medicinally.

modities in the world. Foods that contain chile or its chemical constituents are numerous; they include ethnic foods, meats, salad dressings, mayonnaise, dairy products, beverages, candies, baked goods, snack foods, breading and batters, salsas, and hot sauces.

Chiles are often associated with hot climates, an association that people explain by noting that chiles cause you to perspire, and if you are in a hot climate, that perspiration will cool you off. A more plausible explanation for chiles' association with warm climates is that the chile plant is native to the tropics and grows best in similar climates. Perhaps chiles never caught on in northern Europe because the growing season was too short. Hungarians selected varieties that would grow and fruit in their short growing season and cool climate. Another attribute of chiles is that they have antimicrobial effects, an important benefit in warm climates, where food spoilage is common. The capsaicin and other unidentified antimicrobial compounds in chiles have the power to rid the body of internal parasites that are common in those regions.

Throughout history, the uses of chiles have been as diverse as their colors and shapes: Chiles have been used as currency, tribute, spice, vegetable, ornament, medicine, and to invoke spiritual sensations. During the last two decades, chiles have been the subject of a surge of interest

Throughout history, chiles have been used as currency, tribute, spice, vegetable, ornament, and medicine, and in religious rituals. Today, red chiles are one of the most important spice commodities in the world.

here in the United States. Trade shows, festivals, magazines, Internet web sites, and even an institute are dedicated to the chile. This popularity is due to several factors: First, people have emigrated to the United States from regions such as Southeast Asia and Latin America where chile is an everyday ingredient in food. Chiles are also gaining popularity here because younger people enjoy spicy foods; they relish piquant snacks like buffalo wings, stuffed jalapeños, and chile-flavored corn chips. To satisfy these new cravings, the food industry has embraced spicy foods, delivering many new pungent products. As more safe and reasonably priced fiery foods become available, more people are trying them. And the phenomenon grows: Americans want more flavorful, varied, and healthy food—and chiles deliver.

WHAT MAKES
CHILE PEPPERS
HOT?

PAUL BOSLAND

CONTRARY TO CONVENTIONAL WISDOM, chiles' seeds are not the source of their pungency. Rather, their "heat" is caused by capsaicinoids, alkaloids found only in chiles. Capsaicinoids are located in blisterlike sacs along the fruit's inner wall, or placenta. The sacs break easily when the fruit is cut open or handled roughly, and the capsaicinoids splash onto the seeds.

You can tell, just by looking, how hot a chile will be: Cut open the fruit and look at the walls. If the placenta is bright orange and there are many large sacs, the fruit will be very hot! If there is only a hint of color, the chile will be mild.

The pungency level of any given chile is affected by its genetic make-up, the weather, growing conditions, and fruit age. Plant breeders can selectively develop cultivars within desired ranges of pungency, but any stress to the chile plant will elevate the amount of capsaicinoid in the pods. A few hot days can increase the capsaicinoid content significantly. Planting a sweet chile next to a pungent one will *not* cause the sweet chile to become pungent. But if you save seed from the fruits of the sweet chile for planting next year, the offspring will be pungent if the two plants exchanged pollen and hybridized. This is because pungency is genetically dominant, whereas sweetness is not.

There are 14 known capsaicinoids, among them capsaicin, the most

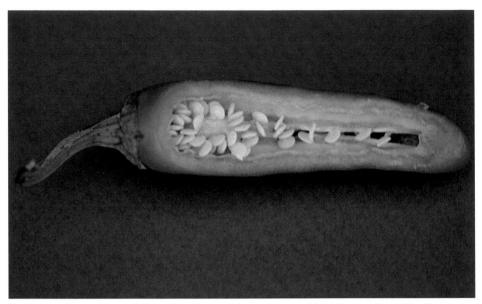

You can tell how hot a chile will be by cutting it open and looking at the walls. If the placenta is bright orange, the fruit will be very hot!

common form. This chemical is so potent that the average person can detect its pungency at a dilution of 10 parts per million.

Chile pungency is expressed in Scoville Heat Units (SHU), named for Wilbur L. Scoville, who invented the scale in 1912. His Scoville Organoleptic Test was the first reliable measurement of the pungency of chiles. This test uses a panel of five human subjects who taste diluted chile extract. Water is added to a sample of extract until the pungency can no longer be detected; this dilution level is used to describe the

DOUSING THE FLAMES

You just accepted that dare and ate a whole habanero. Your mouth is on fire, your heart is pounding, sweat is running down your face, and you're beginning to feel faint. How to extinguish the fire? This is a topic of great debate among chile aficionados. Some claim that plain water is best, while sugar, beer, bread, citrus fruits, tomato juice, and oil all have their advocates.

The latest scientific research, though, says that you should grab a jug of milk and have at it. Milk and milk-based products contain casein, a protein that unbinds the capsaicin—the source of the fire—from nerve receptors on the taste buds. Beans, nuts, and milk chocolate also contain casein, so they may also be effective coolants.

CHILEMAN'S SMOKIN' HOT TURKEY

2 tbsp. apple jelly
1/4 tsp. ground cumin
6 to 12 'NuMex Bailey
   Piquín' chiles, ground
3 to 3 1/2 lb. turkey breast
Cooking oil

Mix apple jelly, cumin, and piquín powder together (jalapeño or habanero-flavored jelly can be substituted). Loosen turkey skin by slipping your finger under skin of turkey breast, pulling it away from meat, but leaving skin attached at one long edge. Place turkey breast, skin side up, on rack in smoker. Use a flavorful hardwood, such as pecan, hickory, or mesquite. Brush skin with oil. Grill until meat thermometer registers 170°F.

Apricot Pineapple Sauce

A nice sauce to serve with the smoked turkey is a mixture of 1 cup of chopped pineapple with 2 pitted and chopped apricots. Add 1 red sweet bell pepper, chopped, and 1/4 cup apple jelly. Mix, cover, and chill in refrigerator until serving time.
—*Paul Bosland*

CARROT-HABANERO SALAD

Its bright, hot colors match the taste of this great salsa.

1/2 habanero chile, seeded,
   finely chopped
1 small clove garlic, finely
   chopped
4 scallions, finely chopped
1/2 cup finely chopped raw
   carrot
1 medium to large tomato,
   seeded, diced, and
   drained
2 tbsp. chopped fresh
   cilantro
1 tbsp. lime juice
Pinch of salt

Combine and chop together all ingredients: Salsa texture should be coarse. If using a processor, process chile and garlic, then add other ingredients and mix briefly. Do not overprocess. Makes 1 cup.

Reprinted with permission from More Recipes From a Kitchen Garden *by Renee Shepherd and Fran Raboff. Copyright 1995 by Renee Shepherd, Ten Speed Press, P.O. Box 7123 Berkeley, CA 94707. Available from booksellers, from www.tenspeed.com, or call 800-841-2665.*

CHILE PEPPER RECIPES

Too pungent for many North Americans, jalapeños are mild when compared to other chiles.

chile's pungency. For example, a 5,000-SHU chile like jalapeño has had 1 part chile extract diluted with 5,000 parts water before the tasters can no longer detect pungency. A more potent chile—say, a 10,000-SHU serrano—would be diluted 10,000 to 1 for the same effect. While these chiles may be too pungent for many North American tastebuds, they're at the mild end of the Scoville scale: Habaneros can score up to 500,000 SHU (see chart, opposite page).

The organoleptic test has limitations. Tasters must be trained and can taste only a limited number of samples before they reach "taster fatigue," when their ability to detect pungency fails. Once widely used, the organoleptic test is being replaced by high-performance liquid chromatography (HPLC). This rapid test quickly processes a large number of chile samples and provides an accurate and efficient analysis of the capsaicinoids present. The instrument "sees" the capsaicinoid molecules and counts them, reporting pungency in parts per million. Pungency is still often expressed in Scoville Heat Units, though, arrived at by multiplying capsaicinoid parts per million by 15.

Like the instrument that performs HPLC, humans can perceive each of the 14 capsaicinoids differently. Different combinations of these capsaicinoids produce the pungency characteristics of individual chile varieties. So, while a habanero may have a sky-high SHU level, its bite isn't necessarily as irritating and persistent as a chile with a lower SHU rating like a Thai pepper.

SCOVILLE HEAT UNITS
OF CHILE VARIETIES AND COMMERCIAL PRODUCTS

100,000-500,000
Habanero
Scotch bonnet
South American *C. chinense*
African birdseye
50,000-100,000
Santaka
Chiltepin
Rocoto
Chinese kwangsi
30,000-50,000
Piquín
'Cayenne Long'
Tabasco
Thai prik khee nu
Pakistan dundicut
15,000-30,000
De Arbol
Crushed red pepper
Habanero hot sauce
5,000-15,000
'Early Jalapeño'
Ají amarillo
Serrano
Tabasco sauce
2,500-5,000
'TAM Mild Jalapeño'
Mirasol
'Cayenne Large Red Thick'

1,500-2,500
Sandia
Cascabel
Yellow wax hot
1,000-1,500
Ancho
Pasilla
'Española Improved'
500-1,000
'NuMex Big Jim'
'NuMex 6-4'
Chili powder
100-500
'NuMex R-Naky'
'Mexibell'
Cherry
Canned green chiles
Hungarian hot paprika
10-100
Pickled pepperoncini
0
Mild bells
Pimiento
Sweet banana
U.S. paprika

From The Pepper Encyclopedia, *by Dave DeWitt, Copyright 1999, by permission of William Morrow & Company, Inc.*

The least irritating capsaicinoid is nordihydrocapsaicin, according to researchers at the University of Georgia. They found that the burning is located in the front of the mouth and palate, causing a "mellow warming effect." The pungency sensation develops immediately after swallowing and recedes rapidly. In comparison, capsaicin and dihydrocapsaicin were found to be more irritating, and were described as having a "typical" pungency sensation. Both compounds produce pungency in the middle of the mouth, the middle of the palate, the throat, and the back of the tongue. In contrast, homodihydrocapsaicin is very irritating, harsh, and very sharp. The pungency does not develop immediately but it affects the throat, back of the tongue, and the palate for a prolonged period.

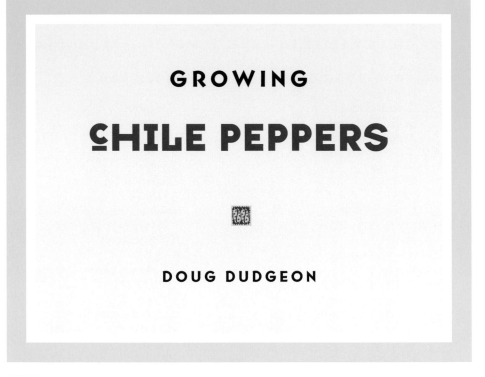

GROWING

CHILE PEPPERS

DOUG DUDGEON

CHILE PEPPERS EVOKE thoughts of spicy foods from hot places—dishes from the Southwest, Mexico, China, India, and Southeast Asia. Perhaps for this reason, many people mistakenly think that the only part of North America where chile peppers will grow is the hot and arid Southwest. But you *can* grow chile peppers just about anywhere in the United States and southern Canada, as long as you prepare your soil, nurture your seedlings properly, and provide the plants with their basic needs.

THE QUIET WINTER MONTHS

Long before you pop your first plant into the ground, you should make a garden plan. You can either grow chiles from seed or buy potted plants closer to planting time. The payoff for using seed is the abundance of varieties—many of them rare and exotic—that seed companies offer. (See "Seed Sources," page 98.) If you decide to grow your chiles from seed, you should start germinating and tending seedlings in the early spring.

If you decide not to grow chiles from seed, you can buy potted plants in the spring from a local garden center or specialty grower. Bear in mind that most garden centers have quite limited selections—often only one to three varieties at most. Specialty growers sell many more varieties of

When choosing chiles to grow, consider how you'll use them. Any chile can be pickled.

Pepper seedlings like tropical conditions.

chile pepper plants, but these are often quite expensive.

Not all varieties do well in every region, so select those that grow best where you live (see "Encyclopedia of Chiles," page 68). But don't be afraid to experiment with offbeat varieties just for the fun of it.

When choosing among chile pepper varieties, keep the following additional factors in mind:

The maturity date for each variety. If you live in a cool, northern climate, your growing season is short, so choose early-maturing varieties. The prolific 'Hungarian Yellow Wax', maturing in 65 days, is a good choice for northern gardens. 'Aci Sivri', an heirloom pepper from Turkey, takes 90 days to mature but fruits abundantly in northern gardens. In contrast, ancho, Anaheim, and chilaca bear quite profusely in the arid Southwest after 90 to 120 days, but do poorly in northern climates.

The humidity in your area. Peppers are sensitive to humidity. Jalapeño, cayenne, and mirasol all prefer arid climates, while habanero, Scotch bonnet, and datil prefer humid surroundings.

How you will use your peppers. Peppers can be eaten raw or prepared in a variety of ways: stuffed with meat or cheese, dried, or pickled. The best peppers for stuffing are large and have thick flesh; poblanos are a good choice and grow especially well in the Southwest. Many of the smaller, thin-fleshed chiles, such as chiltepin, can be dried in the sun, even in climates that lean toward the humid. Any chile pepper can be pickled; jalapeño and pepperoncini are two of the most popular peppers for pickling.

The number of plants you will need. This depends on how many you think you will eat or store. As a rule of thumb, five to six plants of each variety you desire should be more than enough to satisfy a family of four. But find out how much fruit your varieties produce. A single serrano plant can produce up to 50 fruits. Manzano and rocoto will probably bear only a few immature fruits in the Northeast, as they require a long, cool growing season at higher altitudes. In general, the varieties that bear

Chiles require a light, well-drained soil.

small fruits tend to be quite prolific and take less time to mature. A few Thai hot plants, which bear an abundance of small, bullet-shaped fruits, go a long way.

The level of pungency you desire or can handle. The pungency of the different chile pepper varieties is rated in different ways. The simplest rating method is a heat scale of 1 to 10, from mildest to hottest. Pepperoncinis, often used in pickled Italian salads, have little or no heat. The habanero, on the other hand, scores a 10 and is generally considered the world's hottest pepper.

In the "Encyclopedia of Chiles," pages 68 through 97, you'll find detailed descriptions of 57 chile peppers, their preferred growing

HOT CHILES

FOR COOL CLIMATES

These chiles are recommended for areas with short growing seasons:

'Hungarian Yellow Wax'
'Jalapa Jalapeño'
'Long Slim Cayenne'
Superchile hybrid
'Early Jalapeño'
Anaheim
Ornamentals
'Mulato Isleno'

—*Susan Belsinger*

Hold back on water once in a while to make the fruits more pungent.

conditions, heat levels, and tips on how to best grow them. You can also consult "Resources," pages 102 to 104, and seed catalogs. County Extension agents, garden clubs, botanic gardens, and horticultural societies often provide specific regional information.

GERMINATING CHILE SEEDS

Gardeners in most regions should sow seeds 6 to 8 weeks before the last frost. In colder climates, however, you can sow your seed 8 to 10 weeks before the last frost. And if you live in a warm area with a long growing season, you can sow the seed directly into the garden, $1/4$ inch deep, once the soil has warmed to 75°F.

Certain varieties of chile peppers have a seed-coat dormancy and require a treatment to soften the seed coat prior to planting. For example, chiltepins, wild peppers from the Southwest and Mexico, often have a seed-coat dormancy. To soften the coat, soak seed 5 minutes in a 10-percent bleach solution and then rinse. Alternatively, you can soak seeds for 4 hours in a solution of 1 teaspoon saltpeter (potassium nitrate) per 1 quart of water.

Since most chile peppers are tropical plants, if you don't live in a warm region with a long growing season, you'll have to replicate the tropics. (See "The Right Start," page 36.) For most gardeners—those who don't have a heated greenhouse—the best place to start chiles is in a cold frame. Put a thermometer into the cold frame, and if it gets hotter than 80°F, prop open the glass cover. You can also use a heating coil, if necessary, but it's likely that the sun will provide enough warmth.

Fluorescent light stands are another good option for starting pepper plants. However, a sunny window is not a good place to grow seedlings—it is very difficult and should be a last resort.

The potting medium should be light and well drained. Peppers will not tolerate soggy conditions at any stage of their growth. Plastic trays or small peat pots make good containers. When you are ready to sow, first moisten your soil mix, then plant the seed $1/4$ inch deep. (Remember to

WHOLE PICKLED PEPPERS

Carolyn Dille and Susan Belsinger, the authors of Classic Southwest Cooking *(Jessica's Biscuit, 1996), have made good pickled peppers from 'Santa Fe Grande', Hungarian hot, red hot cherry, jalapeño, and serrano chiles.*

1 gallon red, green, and yellow chile peppers
1 quart water
3 cups distilled white vinegar
3 tsp. salt

Wash the peppers. Cut the stems from the large chiles. Make a 1-inch slit with a sharp knife in the larger peppers and a ½-inch slit in the smaller peppers.

Bring the water, vinegar, and salt to a boil in a large enameled or stainless pot. Add the peppers and return to a simmer. Let them simmer for 2 to 3 minutes.

Remove from the heat and pack in hot sterilized jars. Pack peppers to 1 inch from the top and add boiling liquid to ½ inch from the top. Seal the jars.

Process in a boiling-water bath for 25 minutes or in a pressure cooker for 15 minutes. Wrap in towels to cool slowly. The peppers may be eaten immediately, and they will keep until the next season.

—Reprinted with permission of the authors.

PAUL'S PERUVIAN CEVICHE

1 pound very fresh fish filet
Juice of 6 medium limes
2 tomatoes, peeled and
    chopped
1 sweet red or yellow onion
2 tbsp. minced cilantro
2 tbsp. high quality olive oil
1 tbsp. vinegar
Salt and black pepper to taste
2 'Ají Amarillo' chiles, chopped

Cut raw fish into bite-sized pieces and place in a bowl. Pour the lime juice over the raw fish and marinate in refrigerator for 3 to 7 hours, turning the fish occasionally. In ceviche, the lime juice "cooks" the seafood, preserving it. An hour before serving, chop tomatoes, onions, and cilantro; combine and refrigerate. Right before serving, combine olive oil, vinegar, salt, black pepper, chiles, tomato mixture, and fish. Serve with avocado, capers, and corn chips.

—Paul Bosland

CHILE PEPPER RECIPES

GROWING CHILES
NORTH TO SOUTH

Chiles like long, hot days and warm nights. They need warmth and light for germination and early growth, and they flower and set fruit best when days are 8 to 12 hours long and nighttime temperatures are 60° to 70°F. Because they're sun worshippers that like moist soil, planting out chiles can be a bit of a balancing act, especially in the northern regions of the United States and in Canada.

For some general rules of thumb for growing chiles, it is helpful to divide the country into three regions based on frost-free dates and USDA Hardiness Zones (see map, page 106).

THE NORTHERN TIER encompasses Zones 3, 4, and 5. The dates for the last spring frost here have the longest range, from the beginning of May until the end of June. Select chile varieties that mature and fruit within 75 to 80 days (see "Hot Chiles for Cool Climates," page 25).

Since the growing season is short, you need to ensure that your plants have maximum garden time so that they can mature before warm weather ends. Germinate seed indoors about 40 days before you want to transplant the chiles outdoors; they should be just about ready to flower when it is time to set them out. Alternatively, you can buy plants that are already well established.

About two weeks before planting, cover the beds with clear plastic mulch to warm the soil. Harden off the chiles for two weeks (see opposite page). If necessary, plants can be set out early and protected from frost overnight with plastic milk jugs or bottles; remove them each morning. However, it is better to wait until the garden soil is warm, not cold, so that the plants suffer less stress.

Mulching your peppers with black plastic, black mesh, or heavy straw will help the soil retain moisture, keep down the weeds, and reflect sunlight onto the plants, giving them more heat and light.

If cool temperatures come early and your chiles have not yet matured, cover them before dusk with Reemay, lightweight tarps, or even bedsheets. Remove the nighttime covers in the morning before the sun shines too hot and creates an oven beneath the covers.

THE CENTRAL TIER covers Zones 6 and 7. You should have your chile plants ready to set out shortly after the last frost date—early April through mid-May. You can plant them at the same time as you set out basil and tomatoes, when the ground is warming up. If the weather is label your peppers according to variety). Water well, and the seed should germinate in about 10 days. To help prevent diseases, keep the above-ground portion of the seedlings somewhat dry.

When your seedlings put out their second set of leaves, transplant them into larger pots. If you started plants in peat pots, they may remain until planted out. A liquid fertilizer designed for seedlings will give plants a boost; always follow the instructions on the label. As seedlings mature, they will need a little less heat, but watering, air circulation, and lighting must be optimal.

Once the last frost date for your region has passed, you can harden off your plants by moving them

Mulch to control weeds and retain water.

cold—especially if it's wet and rainy—wait to transplant chiles; otherwise, you risk damping off.

In areas of the Central Tier where the soil needs help retaining heat and moisture, it is a good idea to mulch your plants. If all of the fruits are not yet mature at harvest time, you may have to cover your chile plants to protect them from an early fall frost (see above).

THE SOUTHERN TIER includes Zones 8, 9, and 10. This part of the United States is where chiles grow best. The last spring frost in this region occurs sometime during early February to the end of March. As the growing season is long, there is no need to rush the plants into the ground until after the soil has warmed up. Even the peppers that take longest to produce fruit have plenty of time to mature.

The most important thing to watch out for is summer stress during times of high temperature or drought. You needn't be overly vigilant, though—chiles are pretty tough. Just be sure to water and fertilize transplants early on, so that they will be well established before the really hot weather arrives. And bear in mind that if night temperatures are above 86°F, fruit set will not occur.

—Susan Belsinger

Red ripe New Mexico chiles taste fruity.

outside for longer intervals each day. Start by taking them out for a few hours in a shady location, then build up to longer periods in a partly sunny spot. Do this for one to two weeks, bringing plants indoors at night in the early stages. Beware of windy days and intruders such as cats, which can ruin a crop.

PREPARING THE SITE

Before transplanting, it's wise to improve your soil. Humus—thoroughly decayed organic matter—is rich with nutrients that pepper plants need and will also help the soil retain moisture. Supplement your soil with organic matter, especially well-rotted compost, and your plants will become lush and provide you with many more fruits than if you had not amended the soil.

Test your soil to determine its pH. Peppers do best in soil with a pH between 6.0 and 8.0. If the pH is below 6.0, add ground limestone, following the rate of application on the bag. If the pH is above 8.0, you can add peat moss to lower the pH. Thoroughly mix these amendments into the soil.

Plant the peppers in a site that receives full sun at least 6 hours per day. Like most vegetables, peppers will not yield well in a shady location. (One exception is the chiltepin, which is shaded by boulders and the mesquite plant in its native desert areas.)

Choose a site that is protected from high winds, as pepper plants tend to be somewhat brittle. Don't plant them in a plot where you've previously grown members of the Solanaceae or nightshade family—peppers, eggplants, tomatoes, tobacco, potatoes, and petunias—or plants in the Rosaceae or rose family, especially brambles such as blackberries and raspberries. All of these plants can harbor diseases such as verticillium wilt, which infect the soil and then your peppers.

No matter where you live, make sure that your soil is well drained, since peppers will not survive in wet soils. Your planting bed should be level so that the soil has good drainage and water won't pool in depressions. Raised beds work well, but because the soil in them dries out

Harvest green and red Anaheims as soon as they mature to encourage more fruit.

quickly, they're best in areas with good irrigation to offset dry periods, or in wetter climates such as the Northeast. In arid regions, sunken beds work well; place plants in furrows between ridges of soil, where water will collect.

TRANSPLANTING YOUR SEEDLINGS

Whether you bought them or grew them from seed, the plants you put in the garden should be sturdy and have many deep green leaves. Plant them after the last frost date, when daytime temperatures are at least 65° and night temperatures above 55°F. Temperatures any lower will weaken plants, making them susceptible to pest problems and environmental stresses. To give plants good air circulation and room to expand, space them 1½ to 2 feet apart, in rows that are 2 feet apart. Make sure you've properly labeled the different varieties.

Dig a hole a bit wider and deeper than the pot. If you germinated the seed in peat pots, carefully break open the bottom to promote downward root growth. If your plants are in plastic pots, pop out the root ball and gently spread the roots. Put the peat pot or rootball in the hole and fill with soil. The plant's stem should be a bit below the level of the ground. If the plant is elongated and spindly, plant it deeper or sideways and cover a portion of the stem. Rake the planting bed to level out depres-

When a Hungarian wax pepper reaches its ultimate size, it is ready to be harvested.

sions that could trap water.

The most critical factor after transplanting is watering! Water gently and soak the planting bed well, preferably with a hand-held hose. The first few weeks are critical, so water at least daily to ensure that the soil stays moist. Look for wilted plants; this is usually a sign that they need more water, although in some cases they've received too much water. Check the soil. If it's very dry to the touch, increase watering. If your plants are wilting in soggy or saturated soil, either you are overwatering or your plant is suffering from a soilborne disease. (See "Pests and Diseases of Chiles," page 41.)

If you have rich, humusy soil, you may not need to fertilize. Otherwise, you can feed plants with a liquid fertilizer such as 10-55-10 beginning a few weeks after transplanting, and up to once a month during the growing season. Healthy plants are deep green and will begin to flower a week or two after transplanting.

Weeds will undoubtedly sprout among your peppers, and if they remain, they will soon choke out the crop. Cultivate the bed lightly each day, removing all the weeds. Continue watering, and apply a mulch to the soil to keep down weeds and help retain valuable moisture. Use an organic mulch such as straw, wood chips, or pine needles. Cover all soil areas with mulch about 2 inches deep, but don't let the mulch touch the stems of the plants. Use thinner layers in the arid Southwest, where the mulch will not break down as rapidly. You can also use an inorganic mulch, such as black plastic. This is probably the most efficient mulch for weed control, but it absorbs tremendous amounts of heat and makes watering difficult.

MAINTAINING THE PLANTS

Small, compact pepper plants or low-growing ornamental types seldom need staking. However, some plants are taller and bushlike, such as jalapeant ancho, New Mexican, and *Capsicum baccatum* varieties. These plants tend to sprawl due to their height, branching pattern, and fruit

Whether chiles ripen to orange, red, or mahogany, they have the fullest flavor and the most pungency if they're harvested when mature, firm, and evenly colored.

In fall, if there is a threat of frost, remove all peppers, regardless of size.

load, and will fall over, snap, and touch the soil if unstaked. When they begin to sprawl, support them with slender bamboo stakes a bit taller than the plants. Drive three stakes into the ground around the plant, equally distant from each other. Tie garden twine horizontally around the stakes and plant, knotting only to the stakes. Make sure the twine has enough play to support the plant without constricting its growth. If the plants start to look confined, insert a new set of stakes farther from the plants, then carefully undo the original construction.

Chile peppers will often put out shoots that can become leggy. You can cut back the shoots to make the plants grow in a more compact manner. One month after transplanting or after you've staked those plants that need it, remove 4 to 6 inches from all leggy stems with hand shears or scissors, or by simply pinching them off between thumb and forefinger.

Continue watering, but do so less frequently than when the plants were young. Let the soil get a bit dry between waterings; this will help your plants become acclimated to the more adverse conditions. Here in the Northeast, I water no more than twice a week, depending on rainfall. I give the plants a good soaking; in this region, 20 minutes per watering is sufficient. Your plants may show signs of wilting on hot afternoons, but they'll usually recover by the following day if you have taken care of them all along. If you live in an arid climate, you'll have to water more often and more deeply, as your plants will transpire more profusely.

As your chile plants become more established, hold back on watering once in a while. Your plants may suffer a bit but the fruits will become more pungent—because you've stressed your plants, they bite you back more sharply!

Flowering starts as the plants begin to form branches. Peppers are pollinated primarily by bees, which encourage cross-pollination. The resulting fruit will be true to the variety, but its seed will be hybrids, having genetic traits from both parents.

EASY NEW MEXICAN GREEN ENCHILADAS

6 roasted green chiles, chopped
1 can cream of celery soup
Salt, garlic powder, and cumin to taste
1 dozen corn tortillas
1/4 cup canola oil
1 minced onion
Colby cheese, grated

Heat oven to 350°F. Peel, seed, and chop chiles. Add 1/2 can of water to celery soup and bring to a boil. Add chopped chiles. Season to taste with salt, garlic powder, and cumin. Continue to simmer. Dip the corn tortillas into hot oil for a few seconds, turning once with tongs, and drain. Do not overcook, or the tortillas will become tough. Dip the tortillas into the chile and soup mixture. Put a small amount of onions and cheese in the middle of the tortilla and roll up. Place in a casserole dish until full. Pour the remaining chile sauce over the enchiladas. Top with the remaining onion and cheese. Bake for 30 minutes.

—*Paul Bosland*

ENCHANTED JALAPEÑO CORNBREAD

1 1/2 cups stone-ground corn meal
1 tsp. sugar
1/2 cup all-purpose flour
1/2 tsp. salt
1/4 cup shortening
1/2 tsp. baking soda
1 1/2 cups nonfat buttermilk
3 egg whites
2 tsp. baking powder
4 diced pods of 'NuMex Piñata' jalapeño (colored bell peppers or plain green jalapeños can be substituted)

Heat oven to 450°F. Spray 8 × 8 × 2 square pan with nonstick cooking spray. Mix all ingredients; beat vigorously 30 seconds. Pour in pan. Bake 20 to 30 minutes or until golden brown.

—*Paul Bosland*

CHILE PEPPER RECIPES

Chiles can keep producing from one to three months after the first harvest.

THE RIGHT START

Chile pepper seed will germinate best under the following conditions:

· Air temperature of 70 to 80°F
· Bottom heating at 75°F— heated cables work well
· Sterile potting medium
· Good air circulation
· Strong light source
· Proper watering with warm water

Peppers are generally pest-free if you follow good cultural practices. Don't water at night or let the fruits touch the soil, which can harbor disease and pests. If the weather turns very wet, soft rot can infect your plants and cause the fruits to turn to mush. When the weather dries up, your plants usually will improve. Remove any diseased fruits from the garden; don't put them in the compost pile. If you find aphids feeding on the succulent pepper stems, all it takes is a stream of water to knock them off. (See "Pests and Diseases of Chiles," page 41.)

If, early in the season, you leave fruits to develop on plants, you are likely to reduce further flower production. The plant will achieve its ultimate fruit load before you have reached your ultimate harvest. I usually remove as many fruits as possible during the first couple of months after transplanting and then, as the season progresses, I remove larger reddening fruits as needed. Do not leave fruits on your plants past their ripe stage; they are an invitation to diseases such as anthracnose.

HARVESTING CHILES

You can harvest peppers at any time, but generally, when a fruit reaches its ultimate size, it's ready to be harvested. (See "Encyclopedia of Chiles," page 68, and seed catalogs for the maximum size for each variety.) Green peppers are simply unripe; they have a particular flavor that some people prefer. Red peppers are ripe and usually have a fruitier taste. Peppers reach their hottest stage when they are between green and red (or bright orange, in the case of habaneros and Scotch bonnets).

If your peppers don't easily pull free from the plants—and most green peppers won't—simply cut them off using hand clippers or scissors, including as much of the fruit stem as possible. This is especially important if you're storing them.

In the fall, if there is a threat of frost, harvest all peppers regardless of their size, as frost will turn them to mush.

No matter where you live, to ensure continuous flowering and fruiting and to encourage large yields, harvest the first green peppers as soon as they are fully developed. These usually are not as large or hot as end-of-season peppers. Cut the stems about ½ inch above the pepper caps; branches,

Include the fruit stem when harvesting.

especially when they are chile-laden, snap easily. A mature pepper is evenly colored and feels firm. Mature green chile peppers are very good eating; Anaheims and other long green chiles are marketed at this stage. But harvesting a few immature peppers from your garden early is better than having a meager harvest at the end of the season.

Whatever the climate, with good cultivation practices and continuous harvesting, pepper production can last from one to three months after the first harvest. Chiles left on the plant will ripen from green to other colors progressively, showing a rainbow of colors on the same plant. When the chiles ripen to orange, red, or mahogany, they have the fullest flavor and the most pungency.

One final note about harvesting: The "hot" part of the pepper, the capsaicinoids, can burn your skin, especially if you have open cuts. And, the oils (capsaicids) can burn your eyes if you rub them with your fingers. It's best to wear rubber gloves when harvesting, especially if you're sensitive to the oils. The best antidote for burning hands is to rub them with isopropyl (rubbing) alcohol, as the oil is soluble in alcohol.

GROWING CHILE PEPPERS

INDOORS

SUSAN BELSINGER

IT'S A CHALLENGE to grow chile peppers indoors. Like tomatoes, they need an environment that's warmer and brighter than most homes. However, growing chiles indoors is a worthwhile project if you don't have a garden. The best indoor environment for chiles is a greenhouse, of course, but you can also grow them with some success under lights.

An indoor pepper plant will probably never grow as large as one planted outside, and the fruits will most likely be a bit smaller. Selecting plants that grow well in containers will give you the best shot at a good indoor chile crop. The best chiles to grow indoors are the ornamental and smaller hot chiles that are often grown outdoors as container plants. Some chile varieties that grow well indoors and in containers are piquíns, chiltepins, habaneros, and Thai peppers (see "Encyclopedia of Chiles," page 68). These small plants have a long growing season. They fruit and flower for a longer period than short-season chiles, so you will have a greater chance of harvesting fruits from them. The small chiles grow to 6 to 12 inches in height with an equal diameter. Since the peppers stand out prominently above the foliage, these plants make colorful and decorative houseplants. These chiles can be very pungent.

Growing requirements for these smaller, long-season peppers are the

Firecracker chile piquín

'Thai Dragon'

Ornamental pepper

'Fiesta'

same as for other chiles. Outdoors in the southwestern United States where they grow best, chiles like hot daytime temperatures—80° to 90°F plus—and warm nighttime temperatures of about 70°F. To succeed with chile peppers, your home or greenhouse temperatures should be within 20°F of this optimum range. Artificial light, such as a fluorescent tube, placed 3 inches above the plants will raise the temperature by about 10°F. A heat mat beneath the plants will also provide warmth.

The most important factor in growing chiles is light. Just to survive they need at least six hours of bright sunlight a day (southern exposure is best for this) and about eight hours of indirect light (from eastern or western exposure). If you are growing peppers on a windowsill and they appear to be just hanging on, supplement their natural light with artificial light. If you can put your indoor chile plants outside on a porch, balcony,

KEEP THE CHILES COMING

If you have been growing chiles outdoors in the garden and want to pro-long the harvest season, try digging some of the smaller ornamental peppers, potting them, and bringing them indoors. If you have the space and the desire, try to keep some going all year long. They will have a tendency to slow down during the winter months and may lose some leaves and turn a pale green, but do not overfertilize them. Let them rest, consider cutting them back if they get leggy, and look for new growth in the spring.

—Susan Belsinger

or deck for the summer season, this will benefit them enormously.

If you are using only artificial light, your chiles will need 16 hours of light a day, so you might want to place them in an out-of-the-way corner, a closet, or the basement. The plants do need *some* rest, so it's a good idea to set the lights on a timer that turns the lights on and off automatically. You don't have to buy fancy growlights—common fluorescent fixtures with either ordinary cool white or warm white tubes will do. The size and number of fixtures will depend on how many plants you want to grow. You can hang the lights from a ceiling or shelf, or under a work table. Attach chains to the fixtures so that you can easily raise and lower them. Place the lights about 3 inches above the plants and raise them as the plants grow taller, maintaining that 3-inch distance from the plants.

As your chiles grow in their containers, you may have to transplant them more than once. A 10- to 12-inch pot will probably be large enough to grow a small plant to maturity. For larger chiles use a 16- to 18-inch pot. Be sure that your pots have adequate drainage; you'll need a saucer, underliner, or tray on which to place the pots.

Commercial soilless mixes of spaghnum peat or composted bark combined with equal parts of vermiculite or perlite are good for growing chiles. Water the chiles well when you transplant them into a new pot. As they grow, be careful not to overwater them. Keep the plants on the slightly damp to dry side; the medium will turn a lighter color as it dries out. Feed your chiles every three weeks, or according to the fertilizer manufacturer's directions. Kelp and fish emulsion are good organic fertilizers, and granular or concentrated liquids that are mixed with water are widely available and work well.

Chiles will start to mature about 10 to 12 weeks after you have transplant-ed them and will continue to bear fruit for several months. Harvest them when the fruits are shiny and bright green or beginning to turn yellow, orange, or red, depending on the variety. If your chiles appear to be under attack by bugs or pathogens, consult "Disorders, Pests, and Diseases of Chiles" (see next page).

DISORDERS, PESTS & DISEASES OF

CHILES

PAUL BOSLAND

CONTROL OF DISEASE AND PESTS is one of the most important factors in producing a bountiful crop of chiles. Many of the diseases and pests that attack chiles reduce the harvest and the quality of the fruit. Frequent examination of your chile plants will help identify potential threats. Correctly diagnosing the problem is essential so that you choose the proper treatment—and avoid unnecessary and expensive ones.

As a general rule, most pests cannot be eradicated, but they can be managed so that the risk of loss is minimized. The best way to manage pests is to take action before they become serious; after the problem is well established, it is usually difficult to control.

Disease and insect control must start before chile plants and seeds ever reach the garden. Choose disease-resistant chile cultivars (see box on resistant varieties, page 55). Rotate your chile crop to help minimize disease, especially root rot diseases caused by soil-borne pathogens. Space plants properly to provide adequate air movement and help reduce the severity of foliar diseases. In addition, planting healthy seeds and transplants, controlling water in the root zone, getting rid of insects that carry disease, and removing weeds will help you produce an abundant crop of high-quality chiles.

To prevent disease, plant healthy seedlings.

Both nonliving (abiotic) and living (biotic) agents can cause chile disease and injury. Nonliving factors include extremes of temperature, moisture, light, nutrients, soil, pH, air pollutants, and pesticides. Living pathogens that cause disease include bacteria, fungi, mycoplasmas, viruses, insects, and nematodes.

Descriptions, symptoms, and least toxic controls of some of the major abiotic disorders, bacterial diseases, fungal diseases, viruses, and pests affecting chile peppers are listed below. Not all the diseases and pests occur in the same region or at the same time of year.

ABIOTIC DISORDERS

Some abiotic disorders are caused by the lack of a major nutrient such as nitrogen or potassium. Abiotic disorders can also result when certain elements—aluminum, boron, or copper, for example—are overly abundant. These disorders can be similar in appearance to biotic diseases, so carefully investigate the cause of the problem. You can control some of these disorders by avoiding extreme temperatures, inferior soils, and (if possible) air pollutants.

Blossom-end Rot

This disorder first appears as a water-soaked area on the fruit. The tissue near the blossom end of the pods has a brown discoloration. Blossom-end rot in chiles, unlike tomatoes, is never actually at the blossom end of ther fruits. Spots elongate and become brown to black, dry and leathery. Pods affected with blossom-end rot usually ripen prematurely. Wilting, lack of soil moisture, and lack of calcium encourage the problem.

To control blossom-end rot, maintain uniform soil moisture through irrigation and avoid large amounts of nitrogen fertilizer.

Herbicide Injury

Hormone-type herbicides such as 2,4-D, which is commonly found in lawn fertilizers, can cause distorted leaves. Other herbicides may cause chlorosis (yellow, brown, or black areas of dead tissue [necrosis]), or lesions.

FOUR-ALARM CAYENNE CHICKEN

1 1/2 lbs. skinned and boned
    chicken breast, cut into
    2-inch strips
1 tbsp. cornstarch
1 tbsp. soy sauce
1 egg white, slightly beaten
1 clove garlic, minced
Cooking oil
12 dried cayenne chiles,
    halved and seeded

Seasoning sauce:
1 tsp. cornstarch
1/2 tsp. grated fresh ginger, or
    1/2 tsp. dried
1 tbsp. sherry
2 tbsp. soy sauce
1 1/2 tsp. sugar
2 tsp. red wine vinegar
1 tsp. chile paste with garlic
2 tsp. hoisin sauce
3 tbsp. chicken stock
1 tsp. sesame oil
1/2 cup dry roasted peanuts

Prepare seasoning sauce by mixing together ingredients. Set aside.

Place chicken in a small bowl with cornstarch, soy sauce, egg white, and garlic. Mix well. Refrigerate 1/2 hour.

Heat 2 tbsp. cooking oil in a wok or heavy skillet. Add chiles and cook until dark—about 15 seconds. Lower heat, add chicken, and cook about 2 or 3 minutes. Add seasoning sauce and cook another minute. Serve over hot rice, sprinkling peanuts on top. Serves 4.

CANTALOUPE SALSA

1 jalapeño chile, seeded
1 shallot
1 scallion, sliced in 4 pieces
1/2 green bell pepper, cut into
    pieces
1/2 cup cilantro leaves
2 tbsp. lime juice
1/2 cantaloupe, peeled,
    seeded, and cut into pieces
1/8 tsp. salt

In a food processor, combine all the ingredients except cantaloupe and salt. Process until finely chopped. Add cantaloupe and process until cantaloupe is coarsely chopped. (Do not puree.) Add salt and more lime juice to taste. Just before serving, drain off excess liquid. Makes 2 1/4 cups.

Reprinted with permission from Recipes from a Kitchen Garden *and* More Recipes From a Kitchen Garden *by Renee Shepherd and Fran Raboff. Copyright 1993 and 1995, respectively, by Renee Shepherd, Ten Speed Press, P.O. Box 7123 Berkeley, CA 94707. Available from booksellers, from www.tenspeed.com, or call 800-841-2665.*

CHILE PEPPER RECIPES

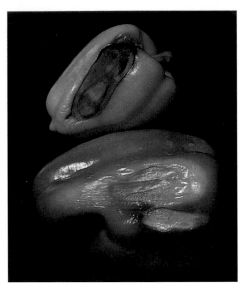

Sunscald affects large-pod green peppers.

Sunscald

Sunscald results when fruits that have been growing in the shade are exposed to too much sunlight. Smaller-podded varieties of chile with erect fruits are not as susceptible as large-podded varieties like bells and New Mexicans. Mature green fruits are more sensitive than mature red fruits. Symptoms include a whitish necrotic area on the side of the fruit exposed to a fierce, usually afternoon, sun.

Keep pods shaded by the plant's leaves or by screening. During harvest, remove as few leaves as possible and keep other damage to a minimum. Avoid stressing the plant.

BIOTIC DISORDERS

Plant pathogens and pests are among the most common causes of reduced yields in chiles. Chile diseases have common names such as root rot, foliar blight, and fruit rot, which typically describe the plant part that is affected; but the most useful criterion for describing a disease is the organism causing the problem.

BACTERIAL DISEASES

Bacterial spot
(*Xanthomonas campestris* pv. *vesicatoria*)
Bacterial spot may be the most serious bacterial disease affecting chiles. On young leaves, it causes small, yellowish green to dark brown, raised spots. On older leaves, the spots are dark, water soaked, and not noticeably raised. When spots are few, they may enlarge to $\frac{1}{8}$ or $\frac{1}{4}$ inch in diameter. The spots appear angular, as the bacteria spreads along the veins. These spots have dead, straw-colored centers with a dark margin. Severely spotted leaves turn yellow and drop. The organism is seedborne and, in some areas, can overwinter on diseased plant debris. Infected seedlings carry the disease to the field, where it can spread rapidly during warm, rainy weather, especially when driving rain and wind have caused injuries to the plants.

Management of bacterial spot depends on a combination of practices.

The most important of these are crop rotation, use of disease-free seed and seedlings, resistant cultivars, and good garden sanitation. Fixed copper compounds are commonly used to help manage the disease, although they are not highly effective under environmental conditions optimal for disease development or when the problem is severe.

Bacterial Soft Rot
(Erwinia carotovora pv. *carotovora)*
Bacterial soft rot affects the fruit. The internal tissue softens, and the pod turns into a watery mass with a foul smell. The disease is most frequent when the weather is hot and humid.

Keep chiles cool, below 70°F. Because the disease can also be started by insect injury, control insect pests.

Bacterial Wilt
(Pseudomonas solanacearum)
Bacterial wilt begins with a wilting of leaves. After a few days, a permanent wilt of the entire plant results, with no leaf yellowing. Test for this bacteria by cutting the roots and lower stems; look for milky streams of bacteria when they are suspended in water.

The best control is to plant clean seed and transplants.

FUNGAL DISEASES
Fungi comprise one of the largest groups of organisms causing diseases among chiles. The most important fungal diseases in the home chile garden are discussed below.

Anthracnose
(Colletotrichum species)
Anthracnose is the common name for the disease caused by several species of fungus in the genus *Colletotrichum*. The disease is most serious on ripe pods. Symptoms are small, water-soaked, shrunken lesions that expand rapidly. The lesions have dark fungal spores in them, and a characteristic concentric ring or target-shaped spot.

Clean seed and crop rotation are important in preventing anthracnose.

Early Blight
(Alternaria solani)
Early blight causes damage to the leaves and the fruit. The disease appears as small, irregular, brown, dead spots, usually on older leaves. The spots, which are ridged and have a target pattern, enlarge until they are $1/16$ to $1/4$ inch in diameter. Early blight is usually more prevalent than anthracnose.

To protect against early blight, plant disease-free seed and seedlings.

Cercospora Leaf Spot
(*Cercospora capsici*)
This disease is also called frogeye. Leaf or stem lesions are oblong or circular with a small, light gray center and dark brown margin, like a frog's eye. The diseased spots usually dry and fall from the leaf, leaving conspicuous holes. Leaf drop is common with severely infected leaves. Stems and fruits are especially susceptible to this disease, which is worst under humid conditions. The environmental conditions that favor this disease also favor bacterial spot. In fact, these two diseases, along with *Alternaria*, are often found together on infected leaves.

Because the disease is seed-borne, planting clean seed and crop rotation are important controls.

Damping-off/Seedling Disease
Several fungi, such as *Pythium, Rhizoctonia*, and *Fusarium*, are associated with this disorder. Seedlings fail to emerge (pre-emergence damping-off), small seedlings collapse (post-emergence damping-off), or seedlings are stunted (root rot and collar rot). Other causes of seedling loss include poor seed quality, improper planting depth, high salt concentrations, a wet seed bed, strong winds, severe nutrient deficiencies or toxicity, pre- and post-plant herbicide applications, and insects.

To prevent seedling diseases, plant only high-quality seed or vigorous transplants and avoid garden beds that are poorly drained.

Gray Mold
(*Botrytis cinerea*)
This fungus causes a sudden collapse of succulent tissues, such as young leaves, stems, and flowers. Gray powdery spore masses occur on the surface of dead plant tissues. High humidity favors the disease.

To ward off gray mold, space plants widely so that they can dry quickly.

Phytophthora
(*Phytophthora capsici*)
This water mold can invade all plant parts and cause at least three separate syndromes: foliar blight, fruit rot, and root rot. It spreads rapidly when humidity and temperatures are high and/or the soil is wet. The first symptom of root rot is severe wilting; within days the plant is dead.

Avoid excess water in the garden. Plant chiles on a high ridge to allow water to drain away from the roots.

Southern Blight
(*Sclerotium rolfsii*)
Southern blight usually occurs during the hot and wet season. It causes plants to wilt as a result of stem girdling and rot at the soil surface—the

base of the stem is brown and decayed above and below the soil line. White fungus is visible at the base of the stem and on the soil around the base. Sclerotia, small brown spheres about the size of mustard seeds, can be found in the fungus.

Cultivate shallowly to avoid scattering soil up on the plants, and remove infected plants promptly.

Verticillium Wilt
(*Verticillium dahliae*)
The symptoms of verticillium wilt are highly variable. Plants may show a yellowing of leaves and a stunting. As the disease progresses, the plants can shed leaves and may finally die. If the stem is cut, a vascular discoloration is visible.

White mold killing pepper plant stems

Crop rotation is the best control. No resistant cultivars are known.

White Mold
(*Sclerotinia sclerotiorum*)
White mold, or sclerotinia disease, causes a wilt, rotting, or blighting of any above-ground or below-ground plant parts. At first, the affected area of the plant has a dark green, greasy, or water-soaked appearance. On stems, the lesion may be brown to gray in color. If the humidity is high, a white, fluffy mold growth appears. Lumpy areas appear in this white growth, which become hard and black as they mature. The hard, black bodies (sclerotia) form inside the stem or on the outside surfaces of the stem and other plant parts.

To guard against white mold, plant chiles in well-drained soil, rotate crops, and carefully remove all infected plants as soon as possible.

VIRAL DISEASES

Some 45 viruses have been reported to infect chiles. Of these, more than half are transmitted by aphids. Viruses alter the plant's cells, causing plants to grow abnormally—leaves may be distorted, abnormally colored, mottled, or curled. Fruit can be mottled, spotted, or shriveled and plants stunted. Leaves, stems, flowers, and fruits may all be affected. One plant can be attacked by many viruses and express many different symptoms.

To protect against tobacco mosaic virus, avoid using tobacco in any form in the garden. Gardeners who use tobacco should wash their hands with soap and water or rubbing alcohol before handling plants. Early detection and removal of infected plants helps, but complete control is often difficult. It may be difficult to distinguish symptoms caused by mosaic diseases from those caused by abnormal soil pH, herbicide injury, nutritional deficiencies, and feeding damage by mites or insects.

To help reduce virus problems, plant virus-free seed, remove weeds, control insects, remove plants showing virus symptoms, and plant resistant varieties. The following practices have also been tried with varying degrees of success, particularly to prevent or reduce viruses transmitted by aphids: organic mulches; aluminum foil strips above the crop; insect traps; mulches of aluminum foil, silver vinyl, or white or translucent polyethylene; aluminum-painted polyethylene sheets; and mineral oil sprays. "Colored baits," sticky sheets of yellow polyethylene spread around the garden, trap the winged form of the aphids and are somewhat effective in controlling the spread of aphid-transmitted viruses. However, planting resistant cultivars is the best way to control viruses, and many virus-resistant cultivars are available. (See box on disease-resistant cultivars, page 55).

INSECT PESTS

The insect problems most common to chile plants are cutworms, aphids, pepper weevils, maggots, flea beetles, hornworms, and leafminers. To control the insect population and keep seedlings insect-free, inspect your plants daily, weed well around the chiles, dispose of diseased plants immediately, and, as a last resort, consider using pesticides.

A cutworm collar protects a chile transplant.

Following are descriptions of the insects and other pests that most commonly attack chiles.

Cutworms

Early in the season, cutworms are the most damaging pests to both seeded and transplanted chiles. There are several species of cutworms; they are the larvae of a large family of moths. They are dull gray, brown, or black, and may be striped or spotted. They are

Black cutworm   European corn borer

stout, soft-bodied, smooth, and up to 2 inches long. When disturbed, they curl up tightly. Cutworms attack only seedlings. They cut off the stems above, at, or just below the soil surface.

Cultivation disturbs overwintering cutworms. To prevent cutworms from reaching young plants, place cardboard, plastic, or metal collars around the stems, pushing the collars 1 inch into the ground. Beneficial nematodes added to the soil in spring or fall will parasitize the larvae.

European Corn Borers
(*Ostrinia nubilalis*)
Corn borer moths are a key pest because they can be found in most every garden every year. To control them, you must target the larval (caterpillar) stage. Moths deposit eggs on chiles, and as they hatch, the larvae tunnel into the chile pod.

Eggs hatch four to five days after being laid, and this is the most appropriate time for control measures. Spray plants with *Bacillus thuringiensis* (*Bt*), sold commercially as Dipel.

Flea beetles
(*Epitrix* species)
Seeded chiles are subject to attack by flea beetles when the cotyledons (the first leaves to appear after seed germination) emerge. These black beetles are about ⅛ inch long. Young plants are severely damaged and full of holes.

Protect young plants with row covers. Give the plants a noontime shower; flea beetles feed at the height of the day, and they don't like to get wet.

Flea beetle

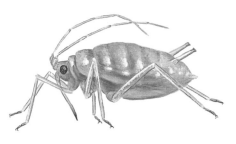

Green peach aphid

Fruitworms

Fruitworms include the fall armyworm, beet armyworm, and tomato fruitworm (corn earworm). At the larval stage, the worms are green, brown, or pink, with light strips along the sides and back. They grow to 2 inches long. The fruitworm damages chile pods by eating holes in them.

Spray plants with *Bacillus thuringiensis* (*Bt*), sold commercially as Dipel.

Green Peach Aphids

(Myzus persicae)

Green peach aphids can become numerous at any time, but are probably more prevalent during the summer. These aphids are usually light green and soft-bodied. They cluster on leaf undersides or on stems, and excrete a sticky liquid called honeydew, which creates spots on the foliage. A black fungus—sooty mold—may then grow on the honeydew and decrease photosynthesis. Severe infestations can cause wilting, stunting, curling, and leaf distortion.

Usually, aphid predators and parasites keep aphid numbers low, but the aphids can multiply quickly. Encourage and release ladybugs and green lacewings into the garden, because they are predators of aphids. An insecticidal soap spray can be used when numbers escalate.

Hornworms

(Manduca sexta and *M. quinquemaculata)*

The worms are the larval stage of the sphinx moth; these large caterpillars have a green body with diagonal lines on the sides and a prominent

CRAB-STUFFED CHILES RELLENOS

Low in calories, rich in flavor.

8 Anaheim, poblano, or
    pasilla chiles
Filling:
1/2 lb. cooked crab meat
2 tsp. fresh lemon juice
1 tsp. hot mustard or 1 1/2
    tsp. Dijon mustard
2 egg whites, lightly beaten
2 tbsp. finely chopped, fresh
    basil
3/4 cup fresh bread crumbs

Preheat oven to 375°F.
    Prepare chiles by roasting
under broiler until tender and
slightly charred. Place in plastic bag to cool for 10 minutes.
Scrape off charred skins with a
paring knife. Slice open one
side and remove seeds. Pat
dry with paper towels.
    Sprinkle crab with lemon
juice. Add mustard, egg
whites and basil, and blend.
Add bread crumbs and toss
mixture together. Open chiles
flat and fill with filling, then
fold chiles together. Place
stuffed chiles on greased baking sheet, cover tightly with
foil, and bake for 20 minutes.
Serves 4 to 6.

GREEN CHILE PEPPER PESTO

*This unusual new dip for chips
keeps 'em coming back for more.*

6 Anaheim, poblano, or other
    mild chile peppers, roast-
    ed, peeled, and seeded
1 jalapeño chile, stemmed
    and seeded
2 cloves garlic, halved
3 tbsp. chopped parsley
3 tbsp. chopped cilantro
    leaves
1/2 cup toasted pine nuts or
    almonds
1 cup freshly grated parme-
    san or asiago cheese
1 1/2 tsp. fresh lemon juice
2 to 3 tbsp. olive oil
Salt and pepper to taste

Combine all ingredients in a
food processor or blender,
adding enough olive oil to
make a thick, smooth paste.
Serve with tortilla chips or
raw vegetables. Serves 6 to 8.

Reprinted with permission from Recipes from
a Kitchen Garden *and* More Recipes From a
Kitchen Garden *by Renee Shepherd and Fran
Raboff. Copyright 1993 and 1995, respectively, by Renee Shepherd, Ten Speed Press, P.O.
Box 7123 Berkeley, CA 94707. Available
from booksellers, from www.tenspeed.com, or
call 800-841-2665.*

CHILE PEPPER RECIPES

Spinach leaf miner   Potato leafhopper

horn on the rear end. They can be up to 4 inches long. They ravenously eat foliage and can strip a chile plant, killing it.

An easy control is to pick off the worms by hand. Alternatively, spray plants with *Bacillus thuringiensis* (*Bt*), sold commercially as Dipel.

Leaf Miners
Many species of flies will cause the leaf-mining disorder. The larva is yellow, about $1/16$ inch long, and lives inside the leaves. The adult is a tiny black and yellow fly. Infected leaves are blotchy. The larvae make long, slender, winding "mines," or trails, under the epidermis of the leaves.

The best method of control for leaf miners is *Bacillus thuringiensis* (*Bt*), sold commercially as Dipel. If damage is minor, treatment is not necessary. Remove infested leaves.

Leafhoppers
Leafhoppers comprise an important group of little sapsucking insects. There are many species of leafhoppers, but the leafhopper *Circulifer tenellus* spreads curly top virus. These are usually green, wedge-shaped, up to $1/8$ inch long, and fly quickly when disturbed. Leafhoppers can cause hopperburn, but it is rare in chiles. The tips and sides of chile leaves turn yellow to brown and become brittle.

Remove infested plants or plant parts immediately.

Pepper Maggots
(*Zonosemata electa*)
The maggot is the larva of a tephritid fly. The slender white or yellowish white maggot is less than $1/8$ inch long. Adults are yellow striped flies

Onion thrips   Greenhouse whitefly

with dark bars on the wings. Maggots feed within the chile pod, causing it to decay or drop from the plant.

Pepper Weevils
(*Anthonomus eugenii*)
The pepper weevil is a severe pest in tropical areas and can cause damage in temperate regions where it has been introduced. The adult feeds on leaves, blossom buds, and pods and will lay eggs on the flowers, buds, and fruit. The eggs hatch and the larvae, white with brown heads, burrow into the young pods, feeding inside the fruit. Premature fruit drop results.

Once the larvae are inside the fruit, practical control is impossible. Preventive measures include destruction of crop residue and weeds of the nightshade family (such as eggplants, tomatoes, and potatoes) to reduce the possibility of adult weevils overwintering. There are no known resistant cultivars at this time.

Thrips
There are many species of thrips and all are extremely small. They can produce a new generation every two weeks. Affected leaves are distorted and curl upward (boat-shaped). The lower surface of the leaves develops a silvery sheen that later turns bronze. The species *Frankliniella tritici* is the vector for tomato spotted wilt virus.

Sulfur and diatomaceous earth are effective against thrips.

Whiteflies
Whiteflies are minute insects with broad wings covered with a fine, white, waxy powder. The immature and adult stages suck plant juices

Root knot nematode   Beneficial nematodes

from the leaves, causing them to shrivel, turn yellow, and drop. In addition, they can carry viruses to chile plants.

Whitefly control is difficult. Good cultural practices, such as removing infected plants, are the best controls.

OTHER PESTS

Spider Mites
(*Tetranychus* species)
Spider mites are red arachnids. When infestation is high, the leaves will have webs on them; if uncontrolled, these mites can kill a plant. Leaves curl downward, like an inverted spoon. Leaves or fruits become bronzed or russeted.

Insecticidal soaps provide some control.

Nematodes
Nematodes can be a serious problem in sandy soils. Symptoms, which vary with plant age and the severity of the infestation, include stunted, nonproductive plants and development of characteristic knots on the plant's roots. Above ground, the plant may be stunted and its leaves wilted. Roots infected with root-knot nematodes may have obvious swellings or galls, varying in size from smaller than a pinhead to larger than a pea.

The best control for nematodes is crop rotation; plant resistant cultivars when available (See box, opposite page.)

DISEASE-RESISTANT CHILES

Listed below is a sample of disease-resistant chile cultivars available from familiar seed companies. It should be noted that seed companies do not always advertise the disease resistance that their cultivars carry. Therefore, it is always worth trying one or two new cultivars in your garden each year. If they do well, add them to your gardening repertoire. If not, try a couple of new ones next year.

NEW MEXICANS
'Anaheim TMR 23'—Virus resistance
'NuMex Joe E. Parker'—Virus resistance

BELL PEPPERS
'Early Crisp Hybrid'—Virus resistance
'Gypsy'—Virus resistance
'Jingle Bells'—Virus resistance
'Jupiter'—Virus resistance
'Keystone Resistant Giant'—Virus resistance
'Lemon Belle Hybrid'—Virus resistance
'Lilac'—Virus resistance
'Little Dipper Hybrid'—Virus resistance
'Lipstick'—Virus resistance
'Oriole'—Virus resistance
'Paladin'—Virus and Phytophthora blight resistance
'Reinger—Phytophthora blight tolerance
'X3R Camelot'—Virus and bacterial leaf spot resistance
'Yolo Wonder A'—Virus resistance

SERRANOS
'Serrano Huasteco'—Virus resistance
'Hidalgo'—Virus resistance

JALAPENO
'Sayula'—Bacterial leaf spot resistance

YELLOW WAX
'Santa Fe Grande'—Virus resistance

PASILLA
'Bajio'—Virus resistance

ANCHO
'Mulato Isleno'—Virus resistance

PIMIENTOS
'Super Red Pimiento'—Virus resistance
'Mississippi Nemaheart'—Nematode resistance

CUBAN
'Quadrato d'Oro'—Virus resistance

CAYENNES
'Mesilla'—Virus resistance
'Carolina Cayenne'—Nematode resistance
'Greenleaf Tabasco'—Virus resistance

CHERRY
'Cherry Bomb'—Virus resistance

—Paul Bosland

PRESERVING

CHILES

SUSAN BELSINGER

IN MIDSUMMER, chile peppers mature, begin to ripen, and become more pungent. Some are fiery hot, while others are crisp, slightly sweet with just a hint of heat, and full of flavor. This is the time to put up that prize-winning corn relish, those pickled peppers, salsas of every kind, and hot pepper chutney.

Depending on the variety, it can take a few weeks for peppers to change color from green to ripe red. Peppers can be eaten no matter what their color, but your preserved chiles will taste best if you use fruits that are all approximately the same level of maturity and color—mature green or ripe red.

Whatever their color, it's always best to wear rubber gloves when working with chiles. Capsaicin, the pungent compound in chiles, can burn your hands, and then your eyes, mouth, nose, or anything else you touch.

Gather jalapeños and serranos while they are still green to make green hot-pepper jelly. Along with tomatoes, tomatillos, and herbs, pick an assortment of hot peppers and preserve a few batches of salsa and relish for the long winter months to come. To tell whether your green peppers are mature, slit one open and look at the seeds. They should be creamy white, big, and flat. If they are brown or not fully developed, the fruit is not yet mature.

Any type of pepper will keep for at least one year in a hot chile herb vinegar.

You can eat red chiles raw, grill them, use them to make red chile jelly, or dry them whole for cooking. Smaller chiles ripen quickly in midsummer, especially Thai and cayenne peppers. Harvest them as they ripen and string them on thin wire to dry; you can then grind them or use them whole as decorations.

ROASTING & FREEZING FRESH CHILES

Green chiles don't dry well but you can preserve them whole by roasting or grilling and then freezing them. (If you freeze them without grilling, the chiles will become mushy.) Large green chiles are best for this method. Most thick-fleshed peppers—New Mexico green chiles, Anaheims, anchos, mulatos, and the sweet bells—have a thin, tough skin that is best removed for pleasant eating. The traditional method is to roast the peppers: They may blacken a little, and the skin will blister and become loose. Once roasted, these chiles will freeze well.

You can roast chiles in three ways, depending on the number you have to prepare. In all cases, cut a small slit at the stem end of the chiles to keep them from bursting. If you only have a few chiles, roast them directly on the open flame of a gas stovetop. Watch them carefully and turn frequently with tongs.

If you want to preserve a larger number of green chiles—say, six or more—place them in a shallow baking pan, and set it about 4 inches below the broiler. Turn frequently to blister the chiles evenly. Watch them carefully so that they don't overcook. The skin does not have to blacken to become loose; if it wrinkles when you push it with the tongs, the chile has been blistered enough.

If you have a large number of chiles to put up, outdoor grilling is an excellent method. The chiles will blister quickly and take on a smoky flavor. Roast the peppers on an open grill over hot coals, about 4 to 6 inches from the flame. Watch the chiles carefully and turn frequently. Roasting peppers usually takes about 4 to 5 minutes for each side, depending on the size of the peppers and the intensity of the heat. Larger peppers will take longer to roast and need to be turned more often. When the chiles are done, the skin should be blistered and charred all over.

As each chile is done, transfer it with tongs to a rack over a baking pan. When all the chiles have cooled to room temperature, place them on a metal pan or a cookie sheet and freeze until they are hard. Transfer the chiles to plastic freezer bags, label and date them, and store them in the freezer.

To use the frozen chiles, thaw them for about an hour. Their skins will slip off easily, and the seed membranes will also be easy to cut after freezing. Chiles taste best and have a fresher texture if you eat them within the first six months. If you remove as much air as possible from the freez-

CHILES RELLENOS

The 'Big Jim' variety of New Mexican chile makes excellent chiles rellenos (stuffed chiles) because the pods are large and meaty, but any of the New Mexican varieties work well in this recipe. Top these chiles rellenos with either green or red chile sauce.

4 green New Mexican chiles, roasted and peeled with stems left on
$1/4$ lb. cheddar or Monterey Jack cheese, cut in sticks
3 eggs, separated
1 tbsp. water
3 tbsp. flour
$1/4$ tsp. salt
Flour for dredging
Vegetable oil for frying

Make a slit in the side of each chile, and stuff the chiles with the cheese sticks. Dredge the chiles with the flour.

Beat the egg whites until they form stiff peaks. Beat the yolks with the water, flour, and salt until thick and creamy. Fold the yolks into the whites.

Dip the chiles in the mixture and fry in 2 to 3 inches of oil until they are a golden brown. Serve with shredded lettuce and guacamole, Spanish rice, and refried beans.

HABANERO PEPPER SAUCE

Cooking the chiles would reduce the distinctive flavor of the habaneros in this hot sauce, so add them raw. The high percentage of both acetic and citric acids keeps the sauce from spoiling.

12 habanero chiles, stems removed, chopped
$1/2$ cup chopped onion
2 cloves garlic, minced
1 tbsp. vegetable oil
$1/2$ cup chopped carrots
$1/2$ cup distilled vinegar
$1/4$ cup lime juice

Sauté the onion and garlic in the oil until soft. Add the carrots with a small amount of water. Bring to a boil, reduce the heat, and simmer until the carrots are soft. Place the mixture and the chiles in a blender, and puree the mixture until smooth. Combine the puree with the vinegar and lime juice and simmer for 5 minutes to combine the flavors.

Strain the mixture into sterilized bottles and seal.

—*Doug Dudgeon*

CHILE PEPPER RECIPES

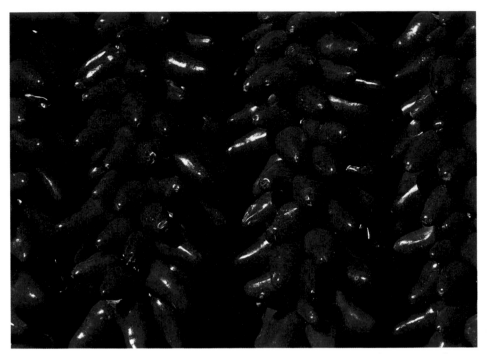

Ristras are chiles tied by their stems with twine and hung in the hot sun to dry.

er bags and have a reasonable freezer, frozen chiles are still quite tasty up to a year later.

If you plan to eat your chiles fresh rather than freezing them, you can peel them by roasting and then steaming them. Put your roasted chiles in a paper or heavy plastic bag, or wrap them loosely in foil to steam the skins loose. Let the peppers steam in the bag for 5 to 10 minutes. Tear open the bag and use it as your work surface so you can keep cutting boards free of chile juice, skins, and seeds. Begin by loosening the skin at the stems where you made a small slit. When the skin is loosened all around the stem, scrape it down with the flat of a knife, turning the pepper as you scrape.

To prepare roasted, skinned chiles for stuffing, cut a slit down the length of the chile, from the stem to about $\frac{1}{2}$ inch from the end. Cut the seed membrane free just under the stem. Parts of the membrane extend down the inner walls; run the knife under these to free the chile of membranes and seeds. Don't worry about a few seeds or blackened bits of skin, and don't rinse your roasted chiles, as this causes them to lose flavor.

If you are not stuffing the chiles, it is easier to simply cut the seed membrane and stem together, even though you lose a little chile flesh. If

Large green chiles are best for roasting, as they blister quickly and take on a smoky flavor.

you simply cut out the pithiest part of the membrane, which holds the seeds, you will not lose much pungency.

Now the chiles are ready for any number of preparations. They can be stuffed, diced, or cut into strips, made into salsa, or canned. (For culinary uses of individual chiles, see "Encyclopedia of Chiles," page 68.) Since the chiles have already been partially cooked, they need little further cooking. For the best flavor, 15 to 20 minutes of cooking are enough for most dishes.

HARVESTING, DRYING, AND SAVING THE SEEDS OF CHILES

Toward the end of the harvest season, when most of the chiles on the plants have matured to red, it is time to pick and dry chiles or to pull the plants and hang them to dry. Pick the peppers while they are still firm and crisp—before they begin to get soft or wrinkly. Red and completely mature chiles will be at their peak of pungency, so wear rubber gloves when working with them.

Keep a close watch on your peppers when they are in their red, ripe stage. If you see any moldy or soft, black spots on the peppers, dispose of them immediately. If the weather is wet, try to harvest the peppers as soon

Roasting Anaheims blackens them, removes the skins, and prepares them for freezing.

as the sunshine dries them, before they begin to mold or rot on the vine.

Dried chiles taste completely different from fresh chiles. They are generally earthier and have a chewy texture. The Southwest is the perfect place for drying chiles. Hot sun, dry air, and warm nights with little chance of precipitation provide the ideal conditions. However, witih a little help from the oven, chiles can also be dried in more humid climates.

Small chiles dry well if you pull the whole plant and hang it upside down in a well-ventilated place. You can also dry smaller peppers by spreading them in a single layer on screens or in large flat baskets, and turn them every day so that they dry evenly. Or, with a needle, you can run a thread through the stems or use a thin wire, and hang them to dry.

Larger peppers with thicker walls take longer to dry. You can spread them on screens or baskets to dry, or make them into ristras—large strings of chiles tied by their stems with heavy string or twine and hung in the hot sun to dry. Ristras are common in the Southwest and Mexico, where these heavy, fat strings of deep red chiles are hung outside from rafters and doorways. Ristras are often used decoratively; if you plan to use them for cooking, once they are thoroughly dried, bring them inside and hang them away from direct sunlight.

If you live in a climate where the temperature and sunlight are uneven

Red chile peppers can be prepared as a sweet and piquant jelly to serve year-round.

and the humidity is high, you can dry your chiles in the sun, but bring them indoors at night or if it rains. Peppers are likely to mold if they get damp or wet during the drying process.

The size of your chiles, the thickness of the flesh, and weather conditions all determine the drying time, which can vary greatly. In the Southwest, where the humidity is low and the sunlight is bright and even, peppers sometimes dry in less than a week.

In humid climates, you can dry chiles partially in the sun and finish them off in a 150° oven; spread them on baking sheets and turn them occasionally. This could take anywhere from 1 to 12 hours, depending on the size and moisture content of the chiles. Feel your chiles to tell if they are thoroughly dried: They should be free of moisture and feel leathery rather than brittle.

Store dried chiles whole in labeled, tightly closed glass jars.

To save chile seed for next year, remove the seed from raw, mature peppers, rinse, and place on paper towels or a small piece of screen. Dry seeds in the sun, in a protected place. When thoroughly dry, pack them into plastic bags, envelopes, or small jars, and label them. Store them in a cool place away from light.

Roast and grind chiles, then mix with herbs to make your own version of chile powder.

GRINDING CHILE FOR SPICES

Pure ground red chile is made from dried chiles and nothing else. This is an essential ingredient in Southwestern and Mexican cooking; it is used in making red sauce for enchiladas, burritos, and huevos rancheros, among other dishes.

To prepare ground red chile, toast the peppers lightly (although tiny chiles like chiltepins and piquíns don't need to be toasted). Use a comal—a large iron griddle for making tortillas—a regular griddle, or a heavy frying pan and toast the chiles over medium heat until they just start to release some fragrance, only about 30 to 60 seconds. Do not over-toast them, or they will have a bitter taste. Stem and seed the chiles, and tear the pods into big pieces. Grind the pieces, about ½ cup at a time, in a food processor or blender. Do the fine grinding in small batches using a spice grinder, coffee mill, or mortar and pestle. Store the ground chile in tightly closed jars away from heat and sunlight. You can also freeze it for up to one year.

Chili powder is different from ground red chile. This American mixture was created in Texas in the late 1800s. Dried chiles are the main ingredient, enhanced by spices and herbs—mainly cumin and oregano, occasionally black pepper, dehydrated garlic, and onions. The original

Many types of chiles can be grilled with other vegetables to make a salsa.

chili powders were pure, without the salt, anticaking agents, or flour that characterize many modern blends.

It's easy to roast your own chiles, grind them as for ground red chile (above), and experiment with herbs and spices to make your own version of chili powder.

Homemade chili powder will keep in a tightly sealed jar out of direct sunlight for six months.

SMALL CHILES AND ORNAMENTALS

Ornamental peppers delight the palate as well as the eye. They add a fiery pungency in cooking and are especially lovely on miniature herb wreaths and kitchen swags, or threaded and hung in miniature garlands. Look for them in seed catalogs under such entertaining names as 'Candlelight', 'Fiesta', 'Fips', 'Fireworks', 'Holiday Cheer', 'Holiday Flame', 'Inferno Mixed', 'Jigsaw', 'Midnight Special', 'Pequin', 'Tepin', and 'Treasure Red'.

You can use these small chiles fresh or, when they ripen to red, you can dry them in baskets and store them in glass jars for future use. Harvesting will stimulate new growth.

All of these little peppers are hot; most of them are fiery. Novices should beware the pungency of these incendiary little peppers.

Because they are so hot, they are most often used whole—simmered in soups or stews, briefly sautéed in stir-fries, or soaked in a marinade—then removed.

VINEGARS AND INFUSIONS

If you have a surplus of the smaller hot peppers, you can pickle them (see recipe, page 27) or, to add new flavors to cuisine, infuse them in vinegar, vodka, tequila, or sherry. Choose fresh, unblemished chiles or small, brightly colored, dried ones. You can use any type of chile in an infusion, but you are sure to succeed with the traditional varieties: serrano, cayenne, jalapeño, 'Santa Fe Grande', red hot cherry, tabasco, Thai, and the ornamentals. Both liquor and vinegar infusions keep for at least one year.

Wash the fresh chiles and make a lengthwise slit in each pepper, fresh or dried, with a sharp paring knife (otherwise they will float like a cork). If you cut the fresh chiles in halves or quarters, there will be more heat in the infusion.

To make a liquor infusion, halve or quarter the chiles and push them down into the neck of the bottle. (You may have to pour out a little bit of the liquor if the bottle is full.) Use two chiles to a half dozen, depending on their heat. I generally use two or three habaneros to a liter bottle of good tequila. Two or three green jalapeños are good for flavoring a bottle of sherry, but I like to put five or six red cayennes or serranos in a bottle of vodka. Do not heat the alcohol. The chiles will float at first, but eventually sink. Allow the infusion to stand for 3 to 4 weeks before using.

Vinegars add zest to salads, sautées, and marinades, and are essential in making *escabeche*, pickled dishes made with vinegar or lime juice. Hot pepper vinegars are made in basically the same way as liquor infusions, except the vinegar is generally heated.

Place your choice of peppers in a large, nonreactive, heavy-bottomed saucepan. If preparing pint jars, use about 1 cup of chiles per jar, and if preparing quarts, use about 2 cups of chiles per jar. Using about $\frac{1}{2}$ cup less liquid than the size of the jar (for example, $1\frac{1}{2}$ cups liquid to a pint jar), pour the vinegar over the chiles. Let the chiles and vinegar come to a boil, reduce heat, and simmer 3 to 5 minutes, then cool to room temperature. Transfer the hot chile vinegar into sterile 1-pint or 1-quart canning jars, leaving about $\frac{1}{2}$ inch of space at the top. You can add a few sprigs of herbs such as thyme, oregano, or sage, if desired. Seal the jars with sterile lids and rings, and set them in a pantry or a cool, dark place for 2 to 3 weeks before using. These infusions become hotter with age.

SHRIMP SAO PAULO

Marinade:
2 tbsp. olive oil
1/2 cup fresh lime juice
1/2 cup dry white wine
2 large cloves finely chopped
  garlic
3 jalapeño peppers, seeds
  and veins removed
1/2 tsp. salt
1/2 cup chopped cilantro leaves

1 1/4 lbs. medium to large raw
  shrimp, peeled and
  deveined
2 tbsp. olive oil
1/4 cup chopped scallions
2 large tomatoes, seeded,
  diced, and drained
Zest of 2 limes

Garnish:
Fresh cilantro leaves

Combine all the marinade ingredients in a bowl. Add shrimp and marinate for just 30 minutes.

In a skillet, heat the additional 2 tbsp. olive oil, add scallions, and sauté until softened. Add drained shrimp (reserving marinade) and sauté quickly for 2 to 3 minutes, until shrimp become firm and turn pink. Add tomatoes and lime zest and heat through. Set aside on a warm platter.

Add reserved marinade to skillet. Cook over high heat for 3 to 5 minutes until marinade is reduced by half. Pour over shrimp on a platter.

Garnish with cilantro leaves. Serve over rice. Serves 4.

Reprinted with permission from More Recipes From a Kitchen Garden *by Renee Shepherd and Fran Raboff. Copyright 1995 by Renee Shepherd, Ten Speed Press, P.O. Box 7123 Berkeley, CA 94707. Available from booksellers, from www.tenspeed.com, or call 800-841-2665.*

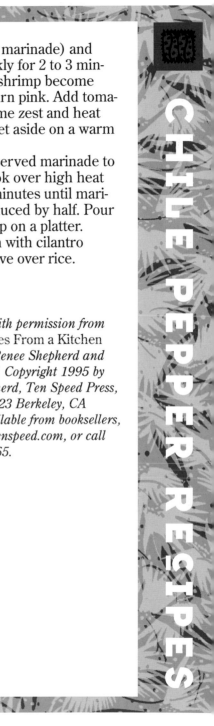

CHILE PEPPER RECIPES

ENCYCLOPEDIA

OF

CHILES

PAUL BOSLAND

There are five species of domesticated chiles—*Capsicum annuum, C. chinense, C. baccatum, C. pubescens,* and *C. frutescens.* Within the first three species, there are numerous pod types, which are distinguishable mostly by their characteristic shape, but can also be differentiated by their use, color, pungency level, aroma, and flavor. Some of the most familiar pod types are the bell, jalapeño, cayenne, New Mexican, pimiento, and yellow wax. Within the pod types are cultivars—cultivated varieties such as 'California Wonder' or 'Early Jalapeño'.

Because they can cross-pollinate, there are thousands of different chiles around the world. This ability to cross-pollinate is an advantage to plant breeders, who can hybridize the many different pod types to create new kinds of chiles. Breeders can cross a yellow bell pepper with a red cayenne, for example, and develop a yellow cayenne or a very hot bell pepper. As plant breeders continue to hybridize and select chiles, gardeners will find an assortment of new chiles that will boggle the mind.

In the following pages, you will find descriptions of more than 50 varieties of chiles, including some new ones such as the pungent bell, 'Mexibell'. You will also find tips on how to grow them in your garden, and how people around the world use them in various dishes. Each chile is also given a pungency rating on a scale of 1 to 10. If you are seeking a fiery thrill, look for the chiles at the high end of the scale.

Capsicum annuum

Capsicum chinense

Capsicum frutescens

Capsicum baccatum

Capsicum pubescens

Capsicum annuum

BELL PEPPER

The bell group has a larger number of cultivars than any other pod group, and is probably the most economically important.

'Jupiter'
'Jupiter', like all North American bell peppers, has fruits that are blocky and about 4″ long and wide; its square shape and flat bottom are preferred for stuffing. Its pods change from green to red as they mature on the plant.
PREFERRED GROWING CONDITIONS: Widely adapted; superb performer in almost every climate.
GROWING TIPS: A very nice, standard bell pepper; disease-resistant and prolific.
CULINARY USES: Excellent for stuffed peppers and fresh in salads.
HEAT LEVEL: 0

'La Rouge'
In Europe, the most popular bell is the elongated 'La Muyo'; in the United States, it is called 'La Rouge'. Its most distinguishing characteristics are the fruit's blossom end, which is more rounded than that of other bells, and 2- to 3-lobed fruits, in contrast to the 4-celled pods of the North American type. The very sweet, thick-walled pods are 6″ to 7″ inches long and about 3½″ wide.
PREFERRED GROWING CONDITIONS: Widely adapted.
GROWING TIPS: Grow as standard bell pepper types.
CULINARY USES: Harvest red, ripe fruits for best flavor.
HEAT LEVEL: 0

'Goldfinch'
The "color revolution" in chiles has been most pronounced among bell peppers. Most grocery stores have green, red, and yellow varieties, and some even sell orange and purple bell peppers. Pepper fruits are purple and green when horticulturally ripe and ready to eat but still physiologically

'Goldfinch'

'Mexibell'

immature. If the pods are left on the plants to mature, they will become red or orange. Fruits may also be yellow, as in the case of 'Goldfinch', which is light yellow, turning deep yellow when mature.

PREFERRED GROWING CONDITIONS: Well-adapted to cool temperatures.

GROWING TIPS: Maintain good foliage cover to protect fruits from sunscald.

CULINARY USES: Excellent in salads or stir-fries, or as a colorful garnish. Cultivars in the colored bell pepper group vary in sweetness; experiment with different cultivars.

HEAT LEVEL: 0

'Mexibell'

This cultivar is unique: It is a pungent bell pepper. Like all bells, it is a compact plant, growing 14″ to 30″ high. A single plant can produce 10 to 20 pods, depending on the season and growing conditions. It is an All-American Selection.

PREFERRED GROWING CONDITIONS: Widely adapted.

GROWING TIPS: Grow as standard bell pepper types. 'Mexibell' will not cause other nearby bell pepper plants to produce hot fruits, but it may cross-pollinate with them and produce seeds for sweet peppers and adding heat to the seeds of regular bells.

CULINARY USES: Makes an excellent, spicy stuffed bell pepper. Also a great way to add a little heat to stir-fries.

HEAT LEVEL: 1

'Gypsy'

An extremely early, sweet, prolific bell pepper; the fruits are elongated, wedge-shaped, 3-lobed, and 6″ to 7″ long. The thick-walled fruits change from greenish yellow to orange red. Up to 18 fruits ripen at once on a compact, 20″ plant. An All-American Selection.

PREFERRED GROWING CONDITIONS: Excellent for short-season areas, but is widely adapted.

GROWING TIPS: A good choice for an early harvest of pods. Resis-

Capsicum annuum

'Gypsy'

tant to tobacco mosaic virus.
CULINARY USES: Flavorful; good fresh, grilled, stir-fried, or in soups and stews.
HEAT LEVEL: 0

'Jingle Bells'

A miniature bell pepper with pods 2″ wide and 2″ to 2½″ long. The young green fruits turn a deep, bright red at maturity. Plants are compact, 20″ tall and 14″ wide. Each plant can set up to 30 fruits.
PREFERRED GROWING CONDITIONS: Widely adapted.
GROWING TIPS: A good choice for container growing. Has plenty of foliage to protect developing fruits.

CULINARY USES: Best eaten when red; the fruits can be stuffed and served as appetizers.
HEAT LEVEL: 0

PIMIENTO

'Pimiento L'

Pimiento, sometimes spelled "pimento," is characterized by heart-shaped, thick-walled fruits that are green when immature and red at maturity. The fruits are nonpungent and the wall flesh is sweeter tasting than most bell peppers. Allspice, *Pimenta dioica*—usually called pimento or

Jamaican pepper outside the United States—is not related to *Capsicum*.

PREFERRED GROWING CONDITIONS: Widely adapted.

GROWING TIPS: Because fruits are harvested when ripe red, can be considered later-maturing than bell peppers. Also, the red fruits are more susceptible to fruit rots. Maintain generous foliage cover to protect against sunscald.

CULINARY USES: Pimiento is used in processed foods such as pimiento cheese and stuffed olives, but can also be eaten fresh in salads.

HEAT LEVEL: 0

'Yellow Cheese'

Capsicum annuum

TOMATO, CHEESE

'Red Ruffles', 'Yellow Cheese'

The fruits of the tomato or cheese type differ from bells and pimiento in that they are generally flat and look like tomato fruits or a cheese wheel. The fruits begin green and turn red, yellow, or orange at maturity. Like bells and pimiento fruits, they are non-pungent.

PREFERRED GROWING CONDITIONS: Excellent for cooler climates; sets well under cool conditions but can be grown in warmer climates.

GROWING TIPS: Some cultivars benefit from staking. Has a continuous fruit set. This is an heirloom type, so plants may not have virus resistance. Fruits may have crackling. Keep soil consistently moist.

CULINARY USES: These peppers are usually pickled, but are also good eaten fresh in salads.

HEAT LEVEL: 0

MUSHROOM

This heirloom variety, also known as "squash," has fruits resembling tiny bells, and may, in fact, be the ancestor of the bell pepper. The fruits start out green

Mushroom, also known as "squash"

and ripen to red, orange, or yellow. Some mushroom cultivars belong to the species *C. chinense* and are related to the habanero; these are very hot!

PREFERRED GROWING CONDITIONS: Widely adapted. Does well in both cool climates and humid, warm summer temperatures. Growing tips: Plants are robust, but there is great variation in plant habit, from spreading to compact.

CULINARY USES: This pungent chile has a fruity aftertaste. It is most often used fresh or pickled, in salads, or as a garnish.

HEAT LEVEL: 2

YELLOW WAX

Fruits are yellow when immature, with a waxy appearance, and turn orange, orange-red, or red at maturity. The fruits can be sweet or pungent. There are two main forms within this group: short-fruited and long-fruited types. The short-fruited types include 'Caloro', cascabella, or yellow wax; 'Floral Gem' is smaller than 'Caloro'. The long-fruited yellow wax type includes 'Sweet Banana', 'Yellow Banana', and 'Hot Banana'.

'Caloro'

'Caloro' and 'Santa Fe Grande' are very similar cultivars. Their habit is usually compact; plants reach a maximum height of 24". The plants are prolific fruit setters. Two or three plants in the garden will provide sufficient fruits for both eating fresh and pickling.

PREFERRED GROWING CONDITIONS: Widely adapted. An excellent choice for difficult chile-growing climates.

GROWING TIPS: Plants are sturdy, compact, and grow well in containers.

CULINARY USES: Mainly a pickle

'Sweet Banana'

Capsicum annuum

type; also a good garnish with a sandwich. Serve as cherry types or, like pepperoncini, as an appetizer.

HEAT LEVEL: 3

'Sweet Banana'

This is a very common cultivar and is nonpungent. However, the 'Hungarian Yellow Wax' types may be pungent. The plants grow to 14″ to 22″ high. The pods are 6″ to 9″ long and turn from yellow to red. Most plants are prolific fruit setters, with up to 25 fruits per plant.

PREFERRED GROWING CONDITIONS: Widely adapted.

GROWING TIPS: Plants benefit from an application of vegetable fertilizer after the first fruit set.

CULINARY USES: The fruits are usually pickled, but can be used fresh in salads or relishes. This is also an excellent choice for pepper steak or rings on a veggie platter.

HEAT LEVEL: 0

HUNGARIAN PAPRIKA

'Feherozon'

Paprika is both a pod type and a product. In the United States,

paprika—any red powder without heat—is a product. Europeans grow Hungarian and Spanish paprika pod types. Hungary produces a wide range of paprikas, from mild to hot, mainly in the regions around Kalocsa and Szeged. 'Feherozon' is one of the most popular cultivars grown in Hungary.

PREFERRED GROWING CONDITIONS: Widely adapted, but does best in moderate climates—neither too hot nor too cold.

GROWING TIPS: Can be grown in containers. Maintain sufficient foliage to reduce sunscald.

CULINARY USES: When fresh, use

Capsicum annuum

'Mississippi Sport'

peach. Because paprika can be made from different pod types, Spanish, Hungarian, and U.S. paprika all taste slightly different.
PREFERRED GROWING CONDITIONS: Does best in warm climates.
GROWING TIPS: Because only ripe red fruits are harvested, needs a long growing season. Supplemental protection such as row covers, plastic, and walls-of-water will all raise fruit production and encourage fruits to mature earlier.
CULINARY USES: Dried and ground. Use as a garnish or a coloring agent, or to add authentic flavor to Romesco sauce.
HEAT LEVEL: 0

as a vegetable. Mature red fruits are dried and then used as a spice. Excellent for adding an authentic flavor to Hungarian goulash.
HEAT LEVEL: 0

SPANISH PAPRIKA

'Bola'
Some Spanish cultivars have a sharp, hot flavor, while others taste mild and sweet. All Spanish paprikas are dark red when mature. 'Bola' means ball, a reference to the round shape of the pod, which is about the size of a

CHERRY

'Sweet Cherry'
Cherry-type pods have small, round, or slightly flattened, immature green fruits that turn red at maturity. As the name suggests, the shape of the pod is similar to that of a cherry. Depending on the cultivar, the fruits are either pungent or not. (Note: An ornamental potted plant, 'Jerusalem cherry' — *Solanum pseudocapsicum*— resembles this pod type but it is not a chile, and its fruits are poisonous.)
PREFERRED GROWING CONDITIONS: Widely adapted.
GROWING TIPS: Some cultivars

have a spreading habit while others are compact. Spreading types can be pruned to make them more compact. (A gradual trimming is better than a one-time, severe pruning.)

CULINARY USES: Same as the yellow wax types. They can be added whole (without the stem) to salads or served on relish trays.

HEAT LEVEL: 0

SPORT

'Mississippi Sport'

'Sport' is a niche chile: It is pickled and served—mainly in the Chicago area—with hot dogs. The cone-shaped fruits are 2″ long, $\frac{1}{2}$″ wide, and very pungent. 'Sport' was supposedly brought to Mississippi by a Swedish farmer, who carried the seeds with him from his homeland. It is also called 'Louisiana Sport'.

PREFERRED GROWING CONDITIONS: Does best in warm climates.

GROWING TIPS: A robust plant, which will nonetheless benefit from additional protection during cold weather.

CULINARY USES: Mainly pickled, but can be chopped fresh to spice up any dish.

HEAT LEVEL: 3

'Corno di Toro'

ITALIAN

'Corno di Toro'

The "bull's horn" is sweet, 5″ to 10″ long and curved like—what else?—a bull's horn. The light green pods ripen to deep red or bright yellow. The fruits are heavy, with moderately thick walls and a sweet, fruity taste. The plant grows to a height of $1\frac{1}{2}$′ to 2′, and is a prolific producer of pods.

PREFERRED GROWING CONDITIONS: Can be grown in cool climates.

GROWING TIPS: Because it is an heirloom, habit varies among

Capsicum annuum

Capsicum annuum

Wild chiltepin

piquíns, bullet-shaped. Plant habit ranges from sprawling to upright.

PREFERRED GROWING CONDITIONS: Needs warm weather to perform its best. It is also a full-season cultivar, taking as long as 100 days to mature.

GROWING TIPS: 'NuMex Bailey Piquín' is an upright, vigorous plant. It can be grown as a perennial in a container.

CULINARY USES: Excellent as a seasoning agent. Use crushed pods in place of salt to season dishes.

HEAT LEVEL: 9

Sinaloa

Many of the chiles in the chiltepin group are harvested from the wild, and the state of Sinaloa, Mexico, has several wild populations of these small, wild chiles.

PREFERRED GROWING CONDITIONS: Needs warm weather; will not grow when temperatures are cool.

GROWING TIPS: Like all chiltepins, Sinaloa is very slow germinating and slow growing. Best to grow in a container and maintain as a perennial.

CULINARY USES: The mature green fruits are pickled, while the red ripe form is dried and used as a seasoning. Don't be fooled by the small size of the fruits—each packs a wallop! Interestingly, the pungency does not linger in the mouth. Folklore also says the

seed sources. Some plants are very tall and benefit from staking.

CULINARY USES: The fresh, crisp flesh is delicious in salads, but more often is sautéed or grilled.

HEAT LEVEL: 0

CHILE PIQUÍN, CHILTEPIN

These chile pods grow naturally in the wild and are the "mother of all chiles"—the evolutionary starting point for all other pod types.

'NuMex Bailey Piquín'

'NuMex Bailey Piquín' is a cultivar developed for machine harvesting. The fruits are very pungent, hotter than most cayennes. A common name for this chile is "bird pepper" because of the fondness birds show for it. The fruits are small, less than 1″ long and ½″ wide, and like those of all

Ancho

pungency of these chiles will not "burn the next day."
HEAT LEVEL: 9

ANCHO

'Ancho 101'

The ancho pod type was developed in pre-Columbian times, and contemporary anchos have retained many of the pod characteristics of the earlier cultivars. Ancho fruits are mildly pungent, heart-shaped, pointed, thin-walled, and have an indented stem attachment. The immature fruits are dark, deep green; they turn red at maturity. The typical ancho pod is 3″ to 6″ long with 2 lobes. Plant height, leaf size, form, and color vary among the ancho cultivars.

There is much confusion regarding the names of ancho fruits: In the fresh state, the green ancho fruits are known as poblanos.

PREFERRED GROWING CONDITIONS: Prefers cool temperatures, around 72°F; will not set well when the weather is hotter than 90°.

GROWING TIPS: A vigorous, tall plant that may need to be staked.

CULINARY USES: Ancho is the chile of choice for making chiles rellenos (stuffed chiles) in Mexico.

HEAT LEVEL: 4

MULATO

'Isleno'

The mulato is very similar to the ancho but matures to a dark chocolate brown instead of red. The fruits are 4″ to 6″ inches long and 3″ wide, tapering to a blunt end. The plant is tall, 3′ to 4′, and sets fruit best when temperatures are cool. The taste has chocolaty overtones.

PREFERRED GROWING CONDITIONS: These are late-maturing and may not ripen to the ultimate brown color in short-season areas.

GROWING TIPS: Multibranched, tall

Capsicum annuum

'Isleno' mulato

PREFERRED GROW-
ING CONDITIONS:
Like their close
relatives the
ancho and mula-
to, these prefer a
moderate cli-
mate.

plants like the ancho. Excessive
fertilizer can cause the plant to
become rangy.

CULINARY USES: Mulatos can be
stuffed like anchos or used in the
dry state to make mole sauce.

HEAT LEVEL: 4

PASILLA

Apaseo
Contributing to the confusion
among names for chiles is that the
mulato is often mistakenly called
pasilla. Pasilla means "little raisin"
in Spanish, so any dried, wrinkled
chile could be called a pasilla.

A true pasilla is a long, slender, dried chile pod. The pasilla
fruits are cylindrical and undulat-
ing. Pods are 6″ to 12″ long and
no more than 1″ wide. They are
dark green, turning brown at
maturity. The pasilla has a raisin-
like flavor with smoky overtones.

GROWING TIPS:
The vigorous, upright plant may
need to be staked. Staking also
keeps fruits from touching the
ground, which will prevent diseases from infecting the pods.
High temperatures will cause
fruit drop. Plants are late-maturing, taking as long as 90 days for
fruits to mature.

CULINARY USES: The fresh green
fruits, chilaca, can be chopped
and added to any dish; the
mature pasilla is dried, then used
in mole sauces.

HEAT LEVEL: 4

CAYENNE

'Charleston Cayenne', 'Large Red Thick'
The young pods of cayenne can
be green, light green, or yellow,
depending on the cultivar, but all
mature to red and are character-
istically wrinkled. The plant is

Cayenne

2½′ to 3′ tall. Pods are 5″ to 10″ long and ½″ to 1″ wide. The pod may be crescent or irregular in shape. It is highly pungent (30,000 to 50,000 SHU).

The cayenne was named either for the city or the river in French Guiana. Historians speculate that the Portuguese may have taken cayennes back to Europe, where they were introduced to India and Africa. It is grown commercially in Africa, India, Mexico, Japan, and in the U.S. in Louisiana, New Mexico, and Texas.

PREFERRED GROWING CONDITIONS: Prefers warm weather, and some cultivars do very well under humid conditions, while others do best in warm, dry climates. 'Charleston Cayenne' was developed by the USDA for the southeastern part of the U.S.; 'Large Red Thick' is the main cultivar grown in the West. Many cultivars will take 90 or more days for fruits to mature.

GROWING TIPS: A versatile choice for the home gardener seeking a spicy, prolific chile.

CULINARY USES: Cayenne is made into a mash with salt for hot sauces, or dried and ground into a coarse powder—the flaked red pepper found in pizza parlors.
HEAT LEVEL: 7

CUBAN

'Cubanelle'
The fruits of the popular Cuban type have large, irregular, thin walls, and a pleasant, mellow flavor. Often known as "frying peppers," 'Cubanelle', 'Biscayne', and 'Aconcagua' are widely grown cultivars, which have only a hint of pungency or none at all. The fruits are elongated, flattened, and yellowish green, changing to red. Plants are of medium height and upright.

PREFERRED GROWING CONDITIONS: Cuban-type chiles prefer warm weather and grow best with less

'NuMex Mirasol'

desalting, the fruits are prepared in a solution of turmeric or yellow coloring and vinegar.

PREFERRED GROWING CONDITIONS: Can be grown in most areas.

GROWING TIPS: The plants grow upright and set fruit well. Continue harvesting fruits to maximize production. After a crop is picked, the plant will begin to reset fruits.

CULINARY USES: Almost always pickled or canned; seldom eaten fresh. Californians now are also grilling the pods and adding them to vegetable dishes.

HEAT LEVEL: 2

foliage cover than most.

GROWING TIPS: Most are early maturing. Fruits ripen about 75 days after transplanting, a little earlier than New Mexican pod types. Provide protection from cold weather so that fruits will set better.

CULINARY USES: This chile is the choice for Mediterranean dishes.

HEAT LEVEL: I

Pepperoncini

The pepperoncini is the well known salad-bar chile. There are two types of pepperoncini: Italian and Greek. Italian has dark green pods. Greek, also called Tuscan, grows in the Tragano region of Greece. The Greek pepperoncinis are medium to light green when picked fresh, but when brined for commercial use, they are treated with sodium bisulfite to remove the green color. After

MIRASOL

'NuMex Mirasol'

The mirasol type has erect fruits, hence its name, which means "looking at the sun." Some of the new mirasol cultivars have pendulate fruits. Pods are 3″ to 4″ inches long, $\frac{1}{2}$″ to $\frac{3}{4}$″ wide, and slightly curved. The pods have a rich, burgundy red color when dried. The plant has multiple stems and branches. Each branch ends with a cluster of fruits.

PREFERRED GROWING CONDITIONS: A full-season cultivar, taking as many as 90 days from transplanting to maturity.

GROWING TIPS: The plant is as wide as tall, so leave a 2′ space around each plant.

CULINARY USES: Mirasol fruits are used only in the dry, red form as chile powder, but they also have ornamental value as an addition to wreaths.

HEAT LEVEL: 4

GUAJILLO

The most characteristic feature of the guajillo is its thin-walled, translucent fruits, which are a rich burgundy color. The guajillo is also known as *pulla* or *chile de comida*—the chile for the kitchen. The pungency dissipates quickly from the mouth. The plants will grow up to 3′ tall, with fruits 5″ long and 1½″ wide at the shoulders.

PREFERRED GROWING CONDITIONS: A full-season type—90 days from transplanting to fruit maturity. Prefers moderate temperatures, neither too hot nor too cold.

GROWING TIPS: Best to transplant to the garden, rather than sowing outdoors. Because the fruit is harvested when red ripe, consider any treatment to reduce high or low temperatures, which will favor earlier ripening.

CULINARY USES: This chile has a distinctive fruity flavor and is the chile of choice for red enchilada sauce.

HEAT LEVEL: 4

Cascabel

CASCABEL

The cascabel is similar in shape to the cherry pepper, but has a thinner wall. The pods are spherical and shiny; when dry they are mahogany to brown in color. The flavor is similar to that of guajillo and mirasol. The dry form of this chile gives the pod its name, cascabel, or rattle—the seeds rattle in the pod of the dried fruits. The cascabel should not be confused with the cultivar 'Cascabella', which is in the yellow wax group.

PREFERRED GROWING CONDITIONS: A full-season maturity type. Prefers a moderate climate, not too hot or cold.

GROWING TIPS: Best started early and transplanted to the garden. Plants are multistemmed and

Capsicum annuum

may need to be staked.

CULINARY USES: The fruits are most often used in the dry form—ground into powder—to flavor fish and shrimp dishes.

HEAT LEVEL: 4

DE ARBOL

The name de arbol is derived from the resemblance of the plant to a tree, although it only grows 2′ to 4′ high. The plant is multistemmed with a tall, straight habit. The fruits are 2″ to 3″ long, very narrow, and translucent when dried. The calyx end of the fruit is narrow and tapered, which distinguishes it from mirasol. The fruits are larger than the chile piquín and are very pungent. Folklore states that the pungency of de arbol does not upset the stomach.

PREFERRED GROWING CONDITIONS: Well adapted to most gardens.

GROWING TIPS: Does well in the garden, maturing in about 80 days after transplanting. The plant can be spreading, so may benefit from staking.

CULINARY USES: The fruits are ground into powder for sauces, soups, and stews. Sometimes fruits are placed whole in jars with vinegar to impart pungency.

HEAT LEVEL: 5

JALAPENO

'NuMex Primavera', 'Jumbo Jalapeño'

The jalapeño was named for the town of Jalapa, Mexico, where it was first marketed. Fruits are thick-walled, conical-shaped, and usually highly pungent. 'NuMex Primavera' is an exception, in that it has only a tenth the pungency of other jalapeños. The majority of jalapeños are medium to dark green, maturing to red. Fruit skin may show a netting pattern, called corkiness; this is considered a desirable trait in Mexico, but undesirable in the U.S.

PREFERRED GROWING CONDITIONS: Widely adapted, can be grown in almost all gardens. Is able to produce bountiful crops in dry or humid, hot or cool climates.

GROWING TIPS: The most common hot chile grown. Compact habit makes it a desirable choice for container growing.

CULINARY USES: Jalapeños are principally used as a spice and condiment; most of the commercial crop is canned or pickled, while a small amount is dehydrated in either the green or red stage. Jalapeños are often used on nacho chips, and are a main ingredient in salsa. Mature red jalapeños are dried by smoking over mesquite or hardwood; the

'NuMex Primavera'

product is called chipotle (which is not a specific pod type of chile).

HEAT LEVEL: 6

'NuMex Piñata'

Most jalapeños are green, maturing to red, but jalapeños of other colors have been developed. The cultivar 'NuMex Piñata' matures from light green to bright yellow to orange and finally to red as it ripens. The plant has light green leaves, and is early and sets fruit prolifically.

PREFERRED GROWING CONDITIONS: Widely adapted, able to set fruit under most conditions.

GROWING TIPS: Early maturing, making it a great choice even in short-season areas.

CULINARY USES: The thick-walled pods of 'NuMex Piñata' make gorgeous salsa and sauces.

HEAT LEVEL: 6

SERRANO

'Huasteco'

This pod type probably originated in the mountains of northern Puebla and Hildago, Mexico, hence its name, serrano, meaning from the highland or mountain. The plants are 3′ high and 1½′ wide. The leaves are very

Capsicum annuum

'NuMex Joe E. Parker'

hairy, giving the plant a silvery appearance. It has cylindrical fruits 2″ to 5″ long and ½″ wide, with medium-thick walls and no corkiness. The immature fruit color ranges from light to dark green. Fruits are red, brown, orange, or yellow when mature.

PREFERRED GROWING CONDITIONS: Does well in most areas, but is adapted to hot, humid climates.

GROWING TIPS: It has an excellent leaf canopy to protect fruits from sun damage, and good disease resistance. Would benefit from protective covers in spring.

CULINARY USES: Serrano is the chile of choice for making pico de gallo, a salsa-type relish.

HEAT LEVEL: 7

NEW MEXICAN

'NuMex Joe E. Parker', 'NuMex Sweet'

The New Mexican pod type was developed in 1894 when Fabian Garcia at New Mexico State University began improving the local chiles grown by the Hispanic gardeners around Las Cruces, New Mexico. The New Mexican pod type is also called long green chile or 'Anaheim'. Actually, the pod type is New Mexican, and 'NuMex Joe E. Parker' and 'Anaheim' are cultivars within this pod type. 'Anaheim' seed originated in New Mexico and was brought to Anaheim, California, where it was widely cultivated. Today, the New Mexican pod type is the basis for the green chile, red chile, and much of the paprika production in the world. Green and red chile represent two developmental states of the same fruit.

PREFERRED GROWING CONDITIONS: Prefers warm weather but can be grown in most locales.

GROWING TIPS: Most are full-season maturity, and benefit from supplemental heating in the spring. Row covers, protective sheets, or walls-of-water will produce an earlier crop.

CULINARY USES: Remove the skins before using. The green pods are roasted and peeled to be eaten fresh, canned, or frozen (see "Preserving Chiles," page 56). The chile of choice outside Mexico for making chiles rellenos. Pungent red pods are usually dried and ground into chile powder, the main ingredient in Mexican-style cooked sauces in the U.S. Paprika is made if the pods are not pungent.

HEAT LEVEL: 4

'Thai Hot'

JAPANESE

'Takanotsume'

This pod type is typical of the pungent chiles from Japan. The fruits are $2^1/2''$ long and $1/4''$ wide, and set in clusters on the plant similar to mirasol types. The fruits are considered hot, but the pungency dissipates rapidly. The translation of takanotsume is "the claw of the eagle," meaning the pungency is sharp.

PREFERRED GROWING CONDITIONS: Will grow in most areas, and has been reported to grow well in New York, Michigan, Florida, California, and Florida.

GROWING TIPS: A vigorous, spreading plant that reaches maturity 80 to 90 days after transplanting.

CULINARY USES: The fruits are used in the red ripe stage, when they are dried and used as a seasoning. This is the typical chile found in pungent soups at Asian restaurants. It is also a nice orna-

mental chile.

HEAT LEVEL: 8

THAI HOT

There are many chiles that are called Thai hot. They originally came from Thailand, but now many chiles from other Asian countries are also called Thai hot. What they all have in common is that the fruits are small and extremely pungent. The fruits range in size from $1''$ to $2^1/2''$ long. The plants are very prolific at fruit setting. The tiny, cone-shaped fruits are borne on very compact plants that also make excellent ornamental houseplants. The pods are used fresh or dried.

PREFERRED GROWING CONDITIONS: Even though it needs warm

Capsicum annuum

'Aci Sivri'

bountiful, producing up to 50 fruits, each about 5″ long.

PREFERRED GROWING CONDITIONS: A good choice for northern gardens, as it is very productive even during cool summer temperatures.

GROWING TIPS: Best to start seedlings early and transplant to the garden. Can take 90 days before the fruits turn red ripe.

CULINARY USES: The fruits are used like cayenne types.

HEAT LEVEL: 'Aci Sivri' is 7; 'Sentinal' is 0.

weather, Thai hot will have harvestable fruits in only 40 days after transplanting.

GROWING TIPS: An excellent choice for growing in containers. Plants are small and compact, and will grow well on a sunny shelf in the kitchen.

CULINARY USES: Fresh pods make a great addition to Asian dishes. The pods can also be dried and stored for winter use.

HEAT LEVEL: 8

TURKISH

Turkey is the second largest producer of chiles in the world, after China. Two common heirloom Turkish cultivars are the pungent 'Aci Sivri' and the nonpungent 'Sentinel'. Both cultivars are

CHIHUACLE

Chihuacle is a rare pod type grown only in southern Mexico. The name suggests domestication was pre-Colombian. Chihuacles vary in shape, but usually measure from 3″ to 5″ in length and from 2″ to 2½″ in width. The fruits are thin-walled; some look like miniature bell peppers, while others are broad shouldered, tapering to a point. Immature fruits are green, ripening to yellow, red, or black—hence the names *chihuacle amarillo*, *chihuacle rojo*, and *chihuacle negro*.

PREFERRED GROWING CONDITIONS: Prefers moderate temperatures.

GROWING TIPS: Protect plants from extreme heat or cold. A tall, multi-branching plant that may need to be staked.

CULINARY USES: The different colored chihuacles are used to produce the unique and famous mole sauces of Oaxaca, Mexico.
HEAT LEVEL: 4

COSTENO

Costeño chiles were originally from Guerrero, Mexico. There is a lot of variability in plant type of the Costeño chile. The plants can grow to 5″ tall, and have many branches starting at the ground level. The pods are long and either conical or oval in shape. They vary in size from 1″ to 6″ long by $\frac{1}{4}$″ to $1\frac{1}{2}$″ wide. The body of the pods is cylindrical and very wrinkled, and some have very deep constrictions in the skin. The outer skin is thin, brittle, and becomes transparent when dried. The pods are predominantly light green or almost yellowish; when they are fully mature they turn light red. They are very pungent.
PREFERRED GROWING CONDITIONS: A moderately well-adapted chile. Prefers dry weather.
GROWING TIPS: If possible, grow where plants are protected from windblown rain.
CULINARY USES: Fresh chopped fruits are added to sauces. The dried pods are ground without seeds to season mole sauces; seeds can be left in the pod when

'Fiesta'

grinding to give the powder a nutty flavor.
HEAT LEVEL: 6

ORNAMENTAL

'NuMex Centennial', 'Fiesta', 'Treasure Red'

Ornamental chiles are a unique group of chiles. Although not really a pod type, they form a distinct group of capsicums. Ornamental chiles are popular in Europe as a potted plant and are gaining in popularity in the U.S. Covered with bright red fruits during the winter holiday season, they are often called Christmas peppers. Although edible, ornamentals are grown primarily for their unusual pod shapes or for their dense foliage and colorful fruits. Ornamental chiles may have all the colors of the rainbow, often displaying pods in four or five colors on a plant at the same time. The plants are very compact and less than a foot high. Most ornamental chiles are pungent but not poisonous.

PREFERRED GROWING CONDITIONS: Widely adapted.

GROWING TIPS: Easy to grow, and many types are perfect for containers.

CULINARY USES: The subtle flavors associated with other pod types is missing in most ornamentals. However, they can be used to spice up a dish. Most have small pods that are very hot.

HEAT LEVEL: 5 TO 10

PETER PEPPER

Seeds of the notorious and naughty heirloom cultivar 'Peter Pepper' have been shared for decades. No one seems to know the origin of the pod. The meaning of the common name is fairly obvious. The pods are very pungent.

PREFERRED GROWING CONDITIONS: Widely adapted.

GROWING TIPS: A robust, vigorous

plant. A fertilizer application after the first harvest will boost subsequent harvests.

CULINARY USES: Some folks pickle them with small white onions and given the concoction to special friends.

HEAT LEVEL: 3

Capsicum chinense

There are myriad pod types within the *C. chinense* species, which originated in the Amazon basin, where the largest diversity in pod type is found. *C. chinense* is now the most common species grown in the Caribbean, where several pod types have been named.

The two most familiar pod types of *C. chinense* are habanero and Scotch bonnet. They differ in pod shape, but the names are sometimes erroneously interchanged. The flavor of the fruits works well with dishes that include citrus.

HABANERO

Red habanero, orange habanero

The habanero pod type is described as lantern-shaped and orange or red at maturity, and is very hot. The habanero chile was originally grown on the Yucatan Peninsula of Mexico and in Belize. The pods can mature to

Red habanero

orange, yellow, white, brown, or red. The pod is $2\frac{1}{2}''$ long and $1''$ wide at the shoulders. The cultivar 'Red Savina' is said to be the world's hottest chile, ranging from 350,000 to 500,000 SHU.

PREFERRED GROWING CONDITIONS: Prefers humid weather.

GROWING TIPS: You may need to provide shelter during cold springs. Most habaneros are late-maturing, so starting transplants early is important. They are also slow-growing when young.

CULINARY USES: The fruits are used fresh in salsas, cooked directly in dishes, or fermented to make a hot sauce.

HEAT LEVEL: 10.

Scotch bonnet

The Scotch bonnet is shaped like a tam-o'-shanter, thus the name. It is grown extensively in Jamaica. Fruits usually mature to yellow, white, red, or orange. A chocolate color is rare. Scotch bonnet is as pungent as the habanero and is the same size. Plants reach a height of $3\frac{1}{2}'$ and have large leaves.

PREFERRED GROWING CONDITIONS: Needs warm to hot growing conditions; handles humid and hot climates well.

GROWING TIPS: Most are late-maturing.Provide similar growing conditions as for habanero (above).

Rocotillo

GROWING TIPS: A full-season cultivar. Start early and transplant. Bottom heat or a growing mat will hasten germination.
CULINARY USES: Used to make relishes and hot sauces. It is also dried and the flakes are used to spice up a dish or as a salt substitute.
HEAT LEVEL: 8

ROCOTILLO

On the island of Puerto Rico and in the West Indies, the most common pod type is the rocotillo. This pod is similar in shape to that of the Scotch bonnet but has a very long pedicel. It is less hot than the standard Scotch bonnet.
PREFERRED GROWING CONDITIONS: Because of its tropical origins, rocotillo is productive only in a warm, sunny location.
GROWING TIPS: A prolific producer of fruits. A light feeding of fertilizer after the first harvest will boost the season's crop.
CULINARY USES: Perfect for seasoning "jerk" meats and to authentically season Puerto Rican dishes.
HEAT LEVEL: 7

CULINARY USES: Similar to the habanero. Summer harvest can be frozen for use in winter. Freezing preserves the fruit's flavor better than canning or pickling.
HEAT LEVEL: 9 TO 10

Datil
The datil is grown around St. Augustine, Florida. It is thought that the datil was introduced to the area by Minorcan settlers in the 1700s, but a more plausible explanation is that it was introduced via trade with the Caribbean islands. The pods are green, maturing to orange or yellow. They are 4" long and 1" wide at the shoulders.
PREFERRED GROWING CONDITIONS: Needs warm growing conditions.

Capsicum frutescens

For reasons that are not understood, the species *C. frutescens* has fewer named cultivars than *C. annuum* and *C. chinense*. It

'Tabasco'

may be that *C. frutescens* grew wild in the same areas as *C. annuum* and *C. chinense*, and that people made selections in those species instead of *C. frutescens*. In Africa and Asia, most chiles that are called "bird pepper" are *C. frutescens*.

'Tabasco'
'Tabasco' fruits are 1″ to 2″ long by ¼″ wide, yellow or yellow green, turning red at maturity, and highly pungent. The 2′- to 3′-tall plants can bear up to 100 erect pods. The yellow, orange, or red fruits make a nice ornamental addition to the garden. The fruits have a unique "dry,"

hot, smoky taste.

PREFERRED GROWING CONDITIONS: Adaptable to most locations. The warmer the location, the bigger and more prolific the fruit set.

GROWING TIPS: Easy to grow; grows well in containers, where the plant can live up to 5 years if protected from frost and cold weather.

CULINARY USES: The red fruits are the ingredient in tabasco sauce and is a major ingredient in creole cooking; gardeners can use 'Tabasco' fresh or pickled.

HEAT LEVEL: 9

'Malagueta'
'Malagueta' is another widespread cultivar, especially in

'Malaqueta'

Capsicum baccatum

The Spanish word *ají* commonly refers to fruits of *C. baccatum* in South America. The Spanish imported to Peru the phonetic word *a´hee* from the native Arawak peoples of the Caribbean. In the Quechuan language of the Incas, chiles are called *uchu*.

'Ají Amarillo', 'Escabeche'

The 'Ají Amarillo' is the most common *C. baccatum* chile in Peru. In the U.S., it is sometimes called yellow Peruvian pepper, even though the fruits are deep orange when mature. The thin-fleshed pods are 5" to 7" long. They have a fruity flavor with berry overtones and a searing, clear pungency. This pod type has been known in Peru since ancient Inca times, and is represented there in drawings and pottery.
PREFERRED GROWING CONDITIONS: Prefers a moderate climate. High temperatures will cause flower drop. Late-maturing, it may take 120 days after transplanting to harvest fruits.
GROWING TIPS: A robust, tall plant, it may need staking. Sensitive to nitrogen fertilizer, so avoid over-fertilizing.
CULINARY USES: This chile is used almost daily in all dishes in Peru, either as a sauce on the plate with other fare or as ingredient in

Brazil. In Africa, where the true melegueta pepper (*Aframomum melegueta*) grows, this *Capsicum* cultivar is called 'Zimbabwe Bird'.
PREFERRED GROWING CONDITIONS: Needs climate similar to that of 'Tabasco' (above).
GROWING TIPS: Seeds are difficult and slow to sprout—it may take 3 to 4 weeks for seedlings to appear. Bottom heat will hasten seed germination.
CULINARY USES: Whole pods can be placed in jars to make spicy vinegar. Dried, the pods are used as a seasoning. Fresh, they can be chopped and used in salsa and other dishes.
HEAT LEVEL: 9

'Ají Amarillo'

Capsicum baccatum

'Christmas Bell'

Capsicum baccatum

the dishes themselves. This chile is the first choice when making ceviche, or marinated fish.

HEAT LEVEL: 5

'Ají Lemon'

Originally from Ecuador or Peru, this fruit ripen from green to a pure lemon yellow. The pod is small and measures 3" to 4" long. When dried, this chile becomes tapered and wrinkled. The fruits have a strong citrus overtone, with a hint of pine woods in the aroma.

PREFERRED GROWING CONDITIONS: Prefers moderate temperatures. Late-maturing.

GROWING TIPS: Transplant after the threat of frost has passed. Avoid high temperatures or too much shade. Needs at least 8 hours of sunlight for best growth.

CULINARY USES: Best used fresh with seafood.

HEAT LEVEL: 8

'Christmas Bell'

Also known as the orchid chile because of its unique shape, this pod type is originally from Brazil, where it is called *ubatuba*. The fruits have a mild pungency and are very flavorful. Plants are vigorous and 30" tall.

PREFERRED GROWING CONDITIONS: Widely adapted. Prefers a moderate climate and conditions similar

to those of anchos and pasilla.
GROWING TIPS: Sow seeds early;
may take 21 days for seeds to
sprout. Transplant when plants
have at least 8 or more true
leaves. Avoid overfertilizing.
CULINARY USES: The pods can be
dried and strung to make a gar-
land for the Christmas tree.
HEAT LEVEL: 4

Capsicum pubescens

This species has numerous local
varieties, grown from the Andes of
Peru to the highlands of Mexico.
It is grown extensively in court-
yards and kitchen gardens. The
pods combine the sweet juiciness
of the bell pepper and the heat of a
habanero. Two main pod types are
manzano (apple-shaped, red) and
peron (pear-shaped, yellow). Also
found are canario (yellow like a
canary), siete caldos (hot enough
to season seven soups), caballo
(the heat kicks like a horse), loco-
to, and rocoto (from the Inca language, Quechuan). The fruits are
used fresh because their thick
walls make them difficult to dry.
The fruits have unique, characteristic black seeds. The plants have
hairy (fuzzy) leaves.
PREFERRED GROWING CONDITIONS:
Late-maturing, these chiles do
best where daily temperatures do
not exceed 80°F. Cannot be
grown outdoors in the desert
Southwest without some protection from the sun.

Manzano

GROWING TIPS: Plants have a
spreading habit and are vinelike.
Use a trellis or staking to keep
plants off the ground. Can be
grown in containers as a perennial. Even though it does best in
cool temperatures, *C. pubescens*
is not frost-tolerant as indicated
in some writings. Some plants
are incapable of self-pollination;
at least two plants are required
for cross-pollination fruit set.
CULINARY USES: Used to season
soups and stews. Fresh pods can
be used to season salsas. If the
fruits are large enough, they can
be stuffed and baked.
HEAT LEVEL: 7

Capsicum pubescens

ALFREY SEED COMPANY
P.O. Box 415
Knoxville, TN 37901
www.freeyellow.com/members2/
hotpep/index.html
Many varieties of chile seeds

THE CHILE WOMAN
1704 South Weimer Road.
Bloomington, IN 47403-2869
(812) 332-8494
www.thechilewoman.net
*More than 200 varieties of open-
pollinated, organically grown chile
peppers; plants only*

CHRIS WEEKS PEPPERS
P.O. Box 3207
Kill Devil Hills, NC 27948
*Dozens of varieties of open-
pollinated seeds*

THE COOK'S GARDEN
P.O. Box 5010
Hodges, SC 29653
(800) 457-9703
http://st6.yahoo.com/cooksgard
en/ index.html
*Small selection of organic chile
pepper seeds*

**CROSS COUNTRY
NURSERIES**
PO Box 170; 199 Kingwood-
Locktown Road
Rosemont, NJ 08556-0170
(908) 996-4646
www.chileplants.com
*Hundreds of varieties; plants only
(no seeds)*

ENCHANTED SEEDS
P.O. Box 6087
Las Cruces, NM 88006
(505) 233-3033
www.tvfuture.com/enchanted
*Specializes in NuMex varieties; has
dozens of others as well*

**HIGH ALTITUDE
GARDENS**
Box 1048
Hailey, ID 83333
(208) 788-4363
www.seedsave.org
*Open-pollinated vigorous seeds
adapted to cold climates and short
growing seasons*

J.L. HUDSON, SEEDSMAN
Star Route 2, Box 337
La Honda, CA 94020
*Small selection of chile seeds, most
un-treated; several unusual
varieties col-lected in Mexico's
Sierra Madre del Sur*

JOHNNY'S SEEDS
Foss Hill Road
Albion, ME 04910-9731
(207) 437-4301
www.johnnyseeds.com
Large selection of hot, sweet, and bell peppers; many varieties for cold-climate gardens

NATIVE SEEDS/SEARCH
526 North 4th Avenue
Tucson, AZ 85705
(520) 622-5561
www.azstarnet.com/~nss/
Heirloom seeds for domesticated and wild chile pepper species

NICHOLS GARDEN NURSERY
1190 North Pacific Highway
Albany, OR 97321
(541) 928-9280
www.gardennursery.com
Sweet and hot chile pepper seeds; several varieties for short and variable season areas

THE PEPPER GAL
Box 23006
Ft. Lauderdale, FL 33307-3006
(954) 537-5540
More than 200 varieties of chile seeds, plus books.

PEPPER JOE'S, INC.
1650 Pembroke Road
Norristown, PA 19403
(410) 628-0507 (fax)
www.pepperjoe.com
Offers a limited selection of organic hot chile pepper seeds

PINETREE GARDEN SEEDS
Box 300
New Gloucester, ME 04260
(207) 926-3400
www.superseeds.com
Specializes in small packets of seeds for home gardeners. Limited selection of chile pepper seeds

PLANTS OF THE SOUTHWEST
Agua Fria
Route 6, Box 11A
Santa Fe, NM 87501
(800) 788-SEED
www.plantsofthesouthwest.com/chiles/
Offers about 30 varieties of chile pepper seeds and plants specializes in those adapted to the Southwest

REDWOOD CITY SEED CO.
P.O. Box 361
Redwood City, CA 94064
(650) 325-7333
www.ecoseeds.com
More than 50 varieties of chile seeds

SANTA BARBARA HEIRLOOM SEEDLING NURSERY

P.O. Box 4235
Santa Barbara, California 93140
(805) 968-5444
www.silcom.com/heirloom/
index.html
Small selection of heirloom chile pepper seedlings.

SEEDS OF CHANGE

P.O. Box 15700
Santa Fe, NM 87506-5700
(888) 762-7333
http://st4.yahoo.net/seedsofchange
Small selection of organic, open-pollinated chile pepper seeds

SEED SAVERS EXCHANGE

3076 North Winn Road
Decorah, IA 52101
(319) 382-5990
Seeds for heirloom and rare varieties of chiles

SEEDS WEST GARDEN SEEDS

317 14th Street N.W.
Albuquerque, NM 87104
(505) 843-9713
www.seedswestgardenseeds.com
Heirloom, organic chile pepper seeds for western gardens

SHEPHERD'S GARDEN SEEDS

30 Irene Street
Torrington, CT 06790-6658
(860) 482-3638
www.shepherdseeds.com
Many unusual, open-pollinated, and heirloom chile seeds

TERRA TIME & TIDE

590 East 59th Street
Jacksonville, FL 32208
(904) 764-0376
www.pepperhot.com
Good selection of chile pepper seeds

TOMATO GROWER'S SUPPLY

P.O. Box 2237
Fort Myers, FL 33902
(941) 768-1119
More than 100 varieties of chile seeds

TOTALLY TOMATOES

P.O. Box 1626
Augusta, GA 30903-1626
(803) 663-0016
Comprehensive offering of chile pepper seeds

TOUGH LOVE CHILE CO.

5025 South McCarran Blvd., #358
Reno NV 89502
(702) 849-3100
www.tough-love.com
Large selection of chile seeds

BOOKS

THE PEPPER GARDEN
by Dave DeWitt and Paul Bosland
Ten Speed Press, 1993

PEPPERS OF THE WORLD:
An Identification Guide
by Dave DeWitt and Paul Bosland
Ten Speed Press, 1996

THE GREAT CHILE BOOK
by Mark Miller
Ten Speed Press, 1991

THE WHOLE CHILE PEPPER
BOOK
by Dave DeWitt
Little, Brown, 1990

PEPPERS: The
Domesticated Capsicums
by Jean Andrews
University of Texas Press, 1995

PEPPERS: A Story of Hot
Pursuits
by Amal Naj
Knopf, 1992

RED HOT PEPPERS:
A Cookbook for the Not so
Faint of Heart
by Jean Andrews
MacMillan, 1993

THE CHILE PEPPER
ENCYCLOPEDIA:
Everything You'll Ever
Need to Know About Hot
Peppers With More Than
100 Recipes
By Dave DeWitt
William Morrow & Co., 1999

THE PEPPER LADY'S
POCKET PEPPER PRIMER
By Jean Andrews
University of Texas Press, 1998

THE HEALING POWER OF
PEPPERS: With Chile
Pepper Recipes and Folk
Remedies for Better
Health and Living
By Dave Dewitt, Melissa Stock, and
Kellye Hunter
Three Rivers Press, 1998

MAGAZINES

FIERY FOODS MAGAZINE
For people in the hot food
business
(505) 298-3835

CHILE PEPPER MAGAZINE
A general-interest magazine
published bimonthly
(888) SPICY-HOT (774-2946)

OTHER RESOURCES

THE CHILE PEPPER INSTITUTE

Box 30003, Dept. 3Q
Las Cruces, NM 88003
(505) 646-3028
(505) 646-6041 fax

www.nmsu.edu/~hotchile/

This clearinghouse for information on chiles publishes the Chile Pepper Institute Newsletter; books on *Capsicum*-related subjects; researches new *Capsicum* cultivars and diseases; sponsors the annual scholarly New Mexico Chile Conference; serves as a bank for chile germplasm.

NATIONAL HOT PEPPER ASSOCIATION

400 N.W. 20th Street
Fort Lauderdale, FL 33311-3818
(954) 565-4972
(954) 566-2208 fax

www.inter-linked.com/org/nhpa/

Trade association for growers, chefs, and companies that produce hot-pepper products, as well as for chile enthusiasts. Publishes a quarterly 28-page newsletter. Membership $20 per year.

CHILES ON THE INTERNET

The Internet is a great source of information for chile gardeners and enthusiasts. Some of the more helpful sites are listed below. Many of these sites are members of "The Ring of Fire," a linked group of web sites that will lead you to more and more information about chiles—as well as a too a lot of chile-related junk. You can also buy chile pepper seeds online, as most of the companies that sell seeds have web sites (see "Seed Sources," pages 98-101). web site addresses change constantly, so you may also want to do your own search for chile information, using a search engine such as Yahoo or Alta Vista.

THE CHILE-HEADS

http://neptune.netimages.com/~chile

A guide to chile pepper recipes, restaurants, and festivals; information about growing, harvesting, and preserving peppers and the botany, chemistry, and medical aspects of chiles. You can also get in on discussions with other chile fanatics, and view archives of exchanges over the past several years.

FIRE GIRL

www.phillips-law.com/home.html

A fun, funky site with information on eating, cooking, worshipping, studying, buying, and growing chile peppers—and lots more.

U.K. CHILE-HEAD

http://easyweb.easynet.co.uk/~gcaselton/chile/chile.html

British chile-head Graeme Caselton has put together a very informative site, with lots of botanical information about the different species and subspecies of chiles, seed suppliers, and a huge database of recipes for chili.

THE FIERY FOODS SUPERSITE

www.fiery-foods.com

This is the site for the people in the pungent food business, but there is lots of interesting information for the gardener as well, including reports from the Annual Chile Conference in New Mexico, where chile pepper researchers present talks about new chiles, chile diseases, etc.

THE PEPPERWORLD HOT SHOP

www.pepperworld.com/hot-shop.htm

Lots of chile pepper chatchkes—posters, calendars, t-shirts, chile pepper cookie cutters, taco racks, de-seeders, clocks, placemats, etc.

LYNN'S PEPPER MUSEUM

www.crl.com/~ledwards/

One gardener talks about her experiences with chile peppers—germinating seeds, when to plant, and so on.

SUSAN BELSINGER is a food writer and photographer. Her work has appeared in publications including *Gourmet*, *Food & Wine*, *Kitchen Garden*, and *Organic Gardening* magazine. She is the coauthor of *New Southwestern Cooking* (MacMillan, 1985), *The Chile Pepper Book* (Interweave Press, 1994), and *Classic Southwest Cooking* (Jessica's Biscuit, 1996). She gives lectures and demonstrations on chiles throughout the United States and Canada.

PAUL BOSLAND is a professor of horticulture at New Mexico State University. He is one of the foremost chile pepper breeders in the world, and is coauthor of *The Pepper Garden* (Ten Speed Press, 1995) and *Peppers of the World: An Identification Guide* (Ten Speed Press, 1996).

DOUG DUDGEON is the assistant horticulturist at the Dawes Arboretum in Newark, Ohio. For nearly 14 years, until early 1999, he worked at the Brooklyn Botanic Garden, where he was in charge of the chile pepper collection, the Japanese Hill-and-Pond Garden, the Fragrance Garden, and the Shakespeare Garden.

BETH HANSON is former managing editor of the Brooklyn Botanic Garden's *21st Century Gardening Series*. She guest-edited the 1997 handbook, *Easy Compost*, contributed to the *The Brooklyn Botanic Garden Gardener's Desk Reference* (Henry Holt, 1998), and writes for various publications about gardening, the environment, and health.

PHOTOGRAPHS

SUSAN BELSINGER: pages 23, 29, 39 (upper left), 62, 63, 64, 65, and 83

PAUL BOSLAND: pages 10, 18, 44, 70, 71, 74, 76, 80, 82, 85, 86, 88, 92, and 94

DAVID CAVAGNARO: pages 12, 13, 15, 16, 20, 24, 26, 30, 42, 47, 57, 60, 61, 73, 77, 78, 79, 81, 87, 91, 93, 95, 96, and 97

DEREK FELL: pages 31, 32, 33, 34, 36, 37, 39 (upper right, lower left, and lower right), 72, and 75

JERRY PAVIA: pages 25 and 89

JUDY WHITE: pages 48 and 72

DRAWINGS

STEVE BUCHANAN: pages 49 (left and right), 50 (left and right), 52 (left and right), 53 (left and right), and 54 (left and right)

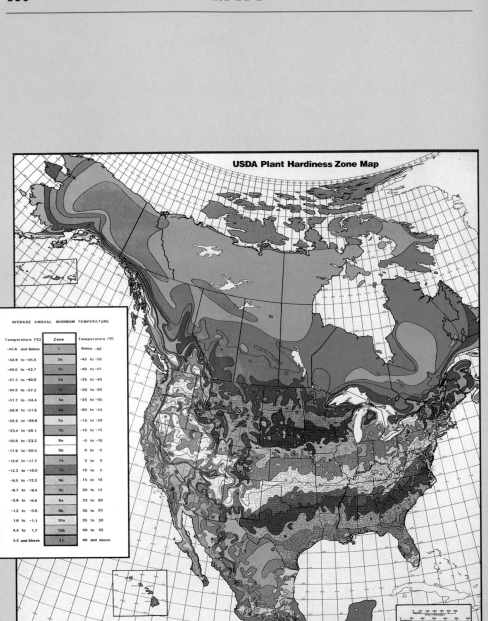

BROOKLYN BOTANIC GARDEN

MORE

BOOKS ON

GOURMET

GARDENING

BROOKLYN BOTANIC GARDEN

handbooks are available at a discount

from our web site

www.bbg.org/gardenemporium

OR CALL
(718) 623–7286